Rob Hunter was 20 when he nine primary school pupils at lived with the terror of those Finally, he has found the wo

Andrew Rule
Journalist (Herald Sun) *and Author*

>>><<<

At last! An insider's account of one of Australia's most sinister crimes.

John Silvester
Journalist (The Age) *and Author*

>>><<<

Friedrich Nietzsche wrote, 'That which does not kill us, makes us stronger.' This rings true for us, the pupils of Wooreen with the challenge of learning to deal with our demons after the trauma.

The ordeal has shaped the lives of each of us impressionable pupils, along with our teacher. It has created a resilient group of individuals, all with a deeper understanding of life that such trauma can bring.

It has led me to a life of community service, desiring to give back to the community, who in the short hours of our abduction rallied in search of us missing Wooreen children.

Ray Argento
South Gippsland Shire Councillor, Mayor 2016/17 and former Wooreen pupil

>>><<<

Rob's story brings us back to that strange event.
Having hauled hundreds of loads of logs along that road
and to meet a speeding vehicle in that exact place at
that exact time was unbelievable. Stuffed my day,
stuffed Eastwood's day worse.

The hardest decision of my life which still haunts me today
was leaving my brother behind when I left the campsite.
All the time running to hopefully get the cops and be back
before Eastwood realised I was missing. It wasn't to be
and so the story goes on. Although we all carry scars
from that event, I thank God that no one was physically
injured. Some divine intervention there I reckon.

Robin Smith
The Truck Driver

DAY 9
AT
WOOREEN

DAY 9 AT WOOREEN

KIDNAPPED WITH NINE CHILDREN...

A TRUE ACCOUNT OF THE CRIME
THAT SHOCKED AUSTRALIA

ROB HUNTER

Foreword by S.I. (Mick) Miller
Former Chief Commissioner
Victoria Police

Published by:
Wilkinson Publishing Pty Ltd
ACN 006 042 173
Level 4, 2 Collins Street
Melbourne, Vic 3000
Ph: 03 9654 5446
www.wilkinsonpublishing.com.au

A catalogue record for this book is available from the National Library of Australia

Planned date of publication: 03-2019
Title: Day 9 at Wooreen
ISBN(s): 9781925642766: Printed – Paperback

Cover design by White Deer Graphic Design
Internal design and typesetting by Tango Media

Photos Courtesy of Victoria Police Museum, Roy Fisher, Joy Butters (Edward), Smokey Oscar, *The Sun News-Pictorial* and John D Pallot

Printed in Australia

DEDICATION

To the Wooreen students of 1977:
You may have been victims; but now you're overcomers.

CONTENTS

FOREWORD

The Wooreen State School Kidnapping

The true story which follows demonstrates that truth can be stranger than fiction. It is Rob Hunter's gripping account of the abduction of the sole school teacher and nine pupils from the Wooreen State School, in South Gippsland, on Monday, February 14, 1977. Rob should know exactly what happened because it was his school. He was that lone school teacher and the nine children were his pupils. It was his first appointment and it was only his ninth day in charge of the little school.

Wooreen was, and still is, a remote, rural area about one hundred and fifty kilometres south-east of Melbourne and some two hours via the South Gippsland Highway. In 1977, its tiny Primary School provided the only educational facility available for the children of local families. As the story unfolds, it will be seen that although being a novice teacher, Rob performed like a veteran during the kidnapping ordeal, doing his utmost to set an example for the children, whose ages ranged from six to eleven, and for whom he was responsible during this diabolical drama.

A strange man entered the school premises that morning, flourishing a gun which he pointed at Rob's chest and threatened to shoot if Rob resisted in any way. What happened next would depend on Rob's reactions and response. He had no reference guide, having to back his own judgment. The children were watching, uncomprehendingly, as their teacher was forced, at gun point, to lie face down on the floor and submit to the further indignity of being handcuffed and chained, and with gaffer tape over his eyes and mouth for much of the time. This was, perhaps, the most critical stage of the abduction of the children and their teacher. Resistance by Rob at this point could have panicked the children as well as the gunman. Fortunately, Rob retained his composure and, in the process, had averted a crisis.

From this point on, when teacher and children were all shackled and loaded into the gunman's vehicle together, Rob had set the example of coolness under extreme stress in the incredible activity that was to follow. Had he not acted with the restraint that he did, the disaster in which they were involved could have become a multiple tragedy at the hand of this agitated gunman.

Later in the day, when parents arrived at the school to pick up their children, they were to discover that teacher and students were not there. The parents soon feared the worst because it was well known that a similar abduction of a teacher and six children had happened at the little State School at Faraday, near Castlemaine, in central Victoria in 1972. And so it proved to be. When local police in Gippsland were advised of the unexpected disappearance of the teacher and pupils from Wooreen, they immediately notified D24 and, as the Assistant Commissioner (Crime) I too was notified. By chance, I happened to have been in charge of the successful initial investigation into the Faraday kidnapping. It soon became apparent to me that the *modus operandi* of the Faraday and Wooreen kidnappings were strangely identical.

While local Gippsland police units were involved in search and pursuit activity, the progress of the activity was being monitored by me as Assistant Commissioner (Crime) back at the Command Centre at Russell Street Police HQ. Frequent media interviews had been given by me and Mr. Lindsay Thompson from the time the abduction became evident. Mr. Lindsay Thompson, who was the Deputy Premier and Minister for Education, participated since he had been nominated in the Faraday kidnapping as the intermediary in the exchange of hostages and the ransom. Media news interviews continued, seeking public cooperation, until 1.45 am.

At 7.15 am the following morning, Tuesday, February 15, 1977, Lindsay Thompson and I proceeded by police helicopter towards the scene of the action. Rob's story gives a thrilling account of the pursuit, during which Eastwood fired a number of shots at the pursuing police units, and his eventual arrest by local detectives. It was all over by the time Mr. Thompson and I arrived.

Later on, Mr. Thompson and I joined with the children and some of their eagerly awaiting family and friends at the Wooreen State School where Mr. Thompson and I both addressed them. And so, the incredible ordeal of the hostages ended. But had it? The hostages — and particularly the children — had been exposed to a protracted, near death experience at the whim of a dangerous psychopath who didn't seem to know what he was doing much of the time. All of the hostages would play and replay the ordeal in their minds over the years, each fighting their own demons. For some, memories could come back to haunt them. But, for now, it was over. They were in the bosom of family and friends. All of the hostages displayed commendable courage and composure for which they can feel justifiably proud.

Some weeks after the release of the hostages, the children were invited to visit Police Headquarters in Russell Street, Melbourne, to see the command and control centre, to let them see what we had been doing while they were hostages. At the conclusion of the visit, one little girl said to me, 'If we get kidnapped again, will you come and rescue us?' I replied, 'Of course we would.' This poignant exchange is my fondest, and most lasting memory of the infamous Wooreen kidnapping.

S.I. (Mick) Miller
AO, LVO, QPM.
Chief Commissioner
Victoria Police
(1977-1987)

INTRODUCTION

Writing, researching and recalling this account of the kidnapping that occurred on February 14, 1977, at Wooreen State School while I was the teacher, has been a deeply emotional experience. I've tried to write the story as if I was there living it again. I've written the drama, through my own eyes, as the events unfolded for me. I've experienced tears, palpitations, anger and a range of emotions that I didn't realise would continue to be evident so long after the initial event. Although I have always been prepared to talk freely about the event, writing it down in much greater detail has meant I've had to delve and dig where it's hurt. I've been reminded of aspects long since forgotten. Feelings and thoughts that I had buried have re-emerged.

Much of the story I had originally overlooked and subconsciously buried: such is the nature of Post-Traumatic Stress. A lot of detail had become misconstrued in my mind. It wasn't until I reread police statements, court case accounts, newspaper articles, looked at police photos and reports, chatted with and questioned many people, revisited the sites and watched video footage of parts of the ordeal that the detail and the correct order of events came back to my memory.

I had often been prompted, by both people and some inner stirrings, to write an account of the Wooreen kidnapping. Thirty-nine years after the event I took the leap of faith.

It came to a head after one of the Wooreen students who I hadn't seen since the event came to visit me in 2015. We talked for a few hours. We both shed tears and expressed some very deep emotions. This seemed to unlock something in me, in a very healthy way, which encouraged me to launch into this writing. Thanks. I am very grateful.

Even with the research, some of the fine detail has remained rather vague. There are still gaps and conflicting information. In some cases, I have had to make 'on balance judgements' to complete the story. Essentially the account is very accurate. However, it is purely through my eyes. My apologies for any mistakes. They are not deliberate.

To preserve their privacy the students' names have been changed.

PART ONE

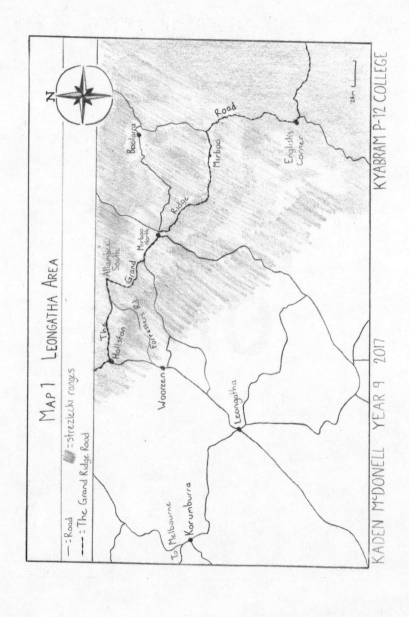

MAP 1   LEONGATHA AREA

— : Road
▓ : Strzelecki ranges
━━ : The Grand Ridge Road

Boolarra

Road

Mirboo

Englishs Corner

Ridge

Allambee South

Grand

Mirboo North

Forresters Rd

The

Hallston

Wooreen

Leongatha

Karumburra

To Melbourne

2km

N

KYABRAM P-12 COLLEGE

KADEN McDONELL   YEAR 9   2017

PROLOGUE
FEBRUARY 14, 1977

I can't see. I can't speak. I can't move.

Blindfolded. Gagged. Bound. Forced onto the floor of a utility.

Driving God knows where.

My nine students are chained up in the back. For fear of being shot, they're lying down flat, out of sight.

We are being driven by a madman with a gun, at a ridiculous speed, on a rough and winding gravel road, going up, down and around. I'm being bounced about like a pinball.

How helpless can you get? What do you do when a bloke threatens to shoot you — and the children you're responsible for — if you don't do what he says?

THE CLASSROOM: 10.30AM

'Mr. Hunter! Mr. Hunter! There's a man outside with a gun!'

I had just let the children outside for recess. Now they were yelling and racing back into the classroom. They looked terrified, faces flushed and words tumbling out.

'He's told us to come back inside!'

'He's got a mask over his head!'

I headed for the front door. Wary of children's tendency to overreact, I expected to meet someone or something trivial. At the back of my mind was a story from one of my teacher's college friends. She had been at a wedding where someone had burst into the reception demanding cash and jewellery from the guests. I wondered for a second if this could be like that — a robbery. But I thought it was more likely, in this farming setting, that it was some harmless hunter out shooting rabbits.

As I stepped through the classroom door into the entry area of my little school, I saw him: a man in a balaclava with a gun in his hand pointed straight at my chest. In his other hand was a red bag.

'Get in and sit down!' he yelled. He pointed back through the door to a chair at the front left of the room.

'Don't try anything fucking smart or I'll shoot you.'

I obeyed. I was twenty years of age.

I had been excited and nervous about teaching at my first school, having my own class of children and putting into practice all that I'd learnt in my three years of training. This was my ninth day in the job and until thirty seconds ago I'd been pleased with the way things had unfolded.

Wooreen was not hard to like — a little dairy farming community in the South Gippsland hills, a few kilometres north of Leongatha. The children were a dream. Cooperative and well behaved, from families who loved them dearly. Their parents were a hard-working and honest lot who had entrusted their children to me, a newly qualified Primary Teacher, with the Education Department of Victoria.

I had met the parents the previous Thursday night at a welcome barbeque. It was a very pleasant evening, settling my nervous concerns regarding parents' uncertainties about both new and green teachers. I was keen to show them I was the right sort of young man and could be trusted to educate their children. I spoke to each of them. It wasn't difficult: there were only six families in the school. Despite my unkempt appearance all the parents were most accepting, friendly and pleasant to the first year out teacher, fresh from college.

The nine students were all brothers and sisters or cousins. Jill and Ron in grades six and five were sister and brother. Leanne, Kay and Russell in grades five, three and two were also siblings. Then there were two sets of cousins, Maggie and Lucy, both in grade six and Bernie and Dale in grades four and two.

Dale was mad about motorbikes. Russell loved machines. Bernie adored horses. Jill was an avid reader. All different in their own ways, all full of potential. They were all so keen to please, eager to impress, willing to work and hungry to learn. I was delighted to get the chance to help them in their paths to adulthood. I was being paid for the privilege of teaching them. It could hardly have been better.

This man with the gun was definitely not part of the plan though.

>>><<<

The gunman was shaking violently and puffing like he'd just done a four hundred metre run. The 'balaclava' was a black and white striped Collingwood football beanie with crudely cut holes for his eyes and nose. The top was also cut out so that it could be pulled further down his face, leaving chunks of his dark hair poking out. The beanie was drawn down over his nose, as far as his top lip, exposing his mouth, chin, lower cheeks and neck.

The children were now all sitting at their desks, having been ordered there by the gunman. Those who had already made it outside for recess had been rounded up by the masked man and brought indoors, the furthest being Russell at the toilet, it seemed. From my seated position I could see all the children. Dale, intent on eating his juicy apple was denied the privilege by this intruder and ordered to leave it on the desk in front of him.

With gun in hand, the gunman stood front and centre of the room, tensely glaring at the children and me.

It seemed like he had been rushing around in a heightened state of excitement for some time. There was an urgency in all his actions. It was like he was late for whatever he had planned. He kept glancing in the direction of the window which faced toward the road, presumably worried about who might happen to come by. He appeared edgy and his presence was extremely scary. I decided that this man, in his nervous and stressed state, holding a firearm, was not to be crossed. My early thoughts were that this guy was probably just a bit crazy and that if I simply did what he asked for a few minutes, that soon enough I would be able to 'get around him' and that he would be appeased. That said, my nerves were kicking into action, my pulse rate was rising, my stomach was tightening, and I was starting to shake inside.

'Don't do anything fucking stupid Teach, or heads will roll,' the gunman said.

Using the F-word in front of school children startled me. It suggested desperation.

'Just do what I say and no one will be hurt,' he continued.

'I'm not a particularly violent man; do what I tell you and you will be okay. I need to tie you all up. It won't hurt. I just have to take you away for a while.'

What? Away? Where to? Tie us up? What are you going to do to us? Will you shoot me? You can't do this. This guy's nuts. Maybe someone will drop in and stop this madness.

The man was still breathing heavily, shaking and looking at us all with flashing eyes through his balaclava. Perspiration was dripping off the lower part of his face — the parts not covered by his balaclava. Coupled with the revolver, our attention was guaranteed. The gun was still being pointed at me.

Who was this guy? I didn't have a clue. With the knowledge of what my friend had gone through at the recent wedding, I thought to suggest options that might satisfy him.

I blurted out, 'I can write you out a cheque. How much would you like?'

I had just become the Headmaster of a one teacher rural school and had little idea how the school accounts worked. I was vaguely aware of extra signatures being required, but I thought it was worth a try. I'd have been happy to empty my own wallet, anything…

'No mate, that's not the sort of money I want,' was the answer.

I wondered what that meant and what sort of money he *did* want. I was reeling, trying to understand what was happening — how this bloke had walked into my new school room, was pointing a gun at me and was ordering us around. I gauged that we had little option other than to do what we were told, for the moment at least.

I looked at the faces of the children sitting at their desks. Confusion. Fear. Puzzlement. I could see them looking at me, watching my reactions, wanting me to do something to stop this absurdity. The older ones were visibly worried by what was taking place. They had spent five to six years in this school growing up with a variety of teachers. This was their school. They had experienced so many things here: normal school routines, concerts, performances, sports days, fairs, working bees, fun times and a whole variety of Wooreen community activities, but not this.

I nodded, trying to look as though everything was fine and quietly complied, giving the children the idea that we didn't have too much to worry about. I thought it was important to display an unruffled disposition.

Look unperturbed.

Keep calm.

Act as if everything is fine.

On the inside though, alarm bells were ringing. Adrenalin pumping. Heart racing. I had a sudden urge to go to the toilet. This scenario wasn't included in any of the teacher training that I had recently completed.

Children being children, the students inadvertently helped to lighten the mood. Leanne, a very cheerful and happy grade five girl, spoke up and asked, 'What's your name?'

The gunman didn't answer.

To help resolve this stalemate, I suggested, 'Perhaps we could call you Joe.'

Not liking that option, he told us to call him, 'Ted'.

My mind raced, along with my accelerated heart rate and adrenalin rush. I needed to do something to short circuit what looked like becoming a desperate situation. In my twenty years on the earth I had sidestepped lots of near calamities. I had run around would-be-tacklers on the football field. I had evaded cows kicking me in the dairy at home, avoided punches from brothers, escaped from various bullies and scary individuals at school. I had avoided and killed snakes and done all sorts of 'heroic things'. Surely I could do something.

But what was facing me now was clearly very different to all the other 'difficult' situations I had overcome. I was the sole teacher. The Headmaster, the PE teacher, the Art teacher, the cleaner, the book keeper... you name it and I was it. Such was the role of the Headmaster of a rural school. Being the only adult, I knew that I had to do something.

Here I was on the ninth day of my teaching career confronted by a desperate man with a gun wanting to tie me and the children in my care up and take us away, and to what end? It was far from clear.

I was now shaking all over.

Thoughts flashed through my head.

Hell! I'll make a phone call if I can. I could make a run for help … No. Not a good idea. I'll write a note. Maybe one of the parents or some other person might turn up and save us. Perhaps one of the kids could make a run for it? Good idea.

Dale was near the door. I thought I'd wait and see if there was an opportunity when the guy wasn't looking. I would get Dale to sneak out the door and make a run for it. As yet I was pretty sure the gunman didn't know the exact number of children there was supposed to be in the room.

I hoped that plan might become a possibility.

The masked man, Ted, was still puffing and panting and looked nervous and distressed. I weighed up his size and my chances of successfully tackling him. He was of medium height with a solid build, considerably thicker set and stronger than me. Attacking this guy alone was not an option I decided, considering his bulk and the gun in his hand. Nor did I think the children should witness their teacher fighting him, and I certainly didn't want the gun going off and harming them in any way.

He was wearing a dark brown sweater and dark blue jeans with a belt. He wore grey gloves. On the back of each glove was a thin strap for tightening or loosening. Each strap was adorned with a red and white star.

He was evidently hot. There was excess perspiration still dripping from the parts of his face that could be seen. It was a strange sight, as it wasn't particularly hot, even though it was summer.

He said, 'Just do what I say and you'll be alright. Kids, if you do anything silly the teacher will get hurt. I'm going to tie you up, starting with Teach here. I don't trust Teach. In fact, I've never trusted any Teach.'

The tying up process began.

'Lie down at the front, on the platform, Teach,' he ordered.

I obeyed. I moved slowly to the front and lay down on my back.

'Not on your back. On your front,' he corrected.

I did as I was told.

'Hold your arms out straight, above your head,' he said.

Rather awkwardly I moved my arms straight out in front of my head on the floor. My forehead rested on the wooden floorboards of the platform. This was a raised area at the front of the classroom. It was about twelve centimetres high and extended across the entire south side of the room, beneath the blackboard.

He took a long chain from his bag. There was the distinct clinking of metal. It was a very clean silver chain — brand new. It was at least ten metres long and reminded me of the dog chains that we had tied up our dogs with on the farm at home. There were even the same clips attached to the chain that we had used to fasten the chain to our dogs' collars.

Then there were the padlocks. A pile of them, all small, some gold, some silver. And keys. All out of the red bag.

Man! What the hell? I don't believe this. I'm about to be chained up like a dog in front of all my students. I'm supposed to be their teacher. I'm supposed to be in charge. I'm supposed to be protecting them. This shouldn't be.

I couldn't comprehend what was happening. It felt surreal. Perhaps it was a game? A game like when I was a child with my brothers? Except this was no made up game. I knew stories of people chained up in slavery and captivity. I'd read about them in books and seen images in movies. But this didn't happen in Australia, in a primary school!

The gunman grabbed my hands roughly and shoved my wrists together. He wrapped the chain tightly around both of my wrists and began to fasten the two links with a padlock. As well as wrapping the chain around my wrists he had to handle a padlock with the corresponding key. Each key and lock had been numbered with a rough hand-written numbering system by a marking pen to match each padlock to its fitting key. The padlock was firstly unfastened, then threaded through two links in the chain that ensured the chain was tight around my wrists — tight enough for my hands not to be able to slip through. His first attempts at doing this were awkward, since he was still shaking. He seemed to take an eternity. The chain was being so tightly and roughly fastened around my wrists that it hurt. I winced. He asked if it was too tight. I agreed, to which he loosened it somewhat, giving me an extra link in the loop around my wrists. I was surprised that he cared, but grateful that he did loosen the binding somewhat.

While the gunman was securing me to the chain, the children asked him questions. Jill seemed to be the major spokesperson. She was in grade six and was a no-nonsense sort of girl, very bright and friendly and had a strong character. All the children loved her.

She asked, 'Ted, what are you going to do with us? Where are you going to take us? How long are we going to be away for? When will we get back?'

Each question was given an off the cuff response. It amounted to us all being taken away for long enough for the gunman's demands to be met — demands which seemed rather vague.

He answered, 'You'll only be away until I get what I want. Don't worry, just do what I say and I won't hurt you. But if you do anything silly, I'll shoot the teacher.'

This dialogue did not seem real.

Shoot the teacher? He couldn't be serious. Not in front of the children. What will happen to the children if he gets rid of me?

I was unsure of what to make of these words. I hoped it wasn't a genuine threat.

Having secured me with the chain and padlock he instructed me to sit back near the children at the front left of the room, on the opposite side of the room from the door, which was our only exit.

I continued to consider some way of escape or some way we could get help or be seen by the outside world. Part of our predicament was that we were largely isolated in our little one classroom school.

The front right of the room had the only door which opened up to the office and entry area — the only orthodox way to exit the classroom and the building. The two side walls of the main room had wooden framed windows that could be opened. They were all about a metre and half from the floor. The west window was a single frame which looked out towards the road and the driveway entrance into the school ground. This was the window that the intruder was particularly concerned with and which I was hoping I would see someone's approach through. The east windows were much larger. However, all that could be seen from them were the numerous large blue gums on the east side of the school ground. My teacher's desk with books and pens and other teacher requirements along with my wallet, watch and keys lay there, beneath this large window. My car, a very old Morris Major that I had recently inherited from my deceased aunt, was parked just outside that window. There didn't seem to be any possibility for help or escape from that direction. The back wall had two high small windows which allowed light in but no visibility to anyone outside. The front of the room, to the south, was dominated by the blackboard.

A message written on the blackboard explaining our plight might be helpful.

The children were still spread around the room sitting at their desks. Dale continued to be on my mind, furthest from me and closest to the door. The gunman remained between me and the children. He was holding the chain while sorting out the padlocks and keys, preparing to fasten the children to the rest of the chain.

He was beginning to speak more sensibly, more slowly and to act in less of a crazed state. His agitation was abating. His breathing was becoming more normal and he was no longer sweating profusely. Some semblance of order was emerging as we obeyed this man's commands.

I continued to look for an opportunity to stop this ridiculous situation.

Once the gunman had his next padlock and key ready he asked, 'Okay, now who would like to go first? Who would like to be tied up next to Teach?'

Russell, a very eager child full of bravado volunteered. Russell was one of the younger children and was only six years old. In essence, I think he thought this process was some sort of game. He was instructed to come over and join me. The gunman then looped and padlocked the chain around Russell's left wrist, a little less than a metre along the chain from where my two wrists were fastened.

The rest of the children and I watched. Although Russell might not have understood what was really happening, most of the other children certainly did. They watched on with anxious faces glancing at each other, at the gunman and at me, trying to work out 'what the story was'. There was a mixture of fear and puzzlement in their looks. The older ones in particular showed serious concern.

They must have been totally bewildered by these proceedings. A hooded intruder wielding a gun had entered their domain, chained up their teacher and was about to do the same to them. It couldn't be real. Any moment it would all stop or someone would come and rescue them.

Once the chain was secured around Russell's wrist, the gunman worked at unlocking the next padlock with the correct key to chain up Kay, who was sitting right by me. While he was securing the chain to Kay's wrist, he was leaning over with his backside towards me. In his back pocket was the gun, easily within my reach.

The gun looked much like the cap guns I had played cops and robbers with as a child. One of the children later described the gun as 'looking like a cowboy gun'. My experience with real firearms was limited to the few occasions I'd unsuccessfully attempted to shoot a crow or two with Dad's rifle. To my untrained eye, the gun that I now gazed at was not totally dissimilar to my toy gun.

I thought I could grab the gun. Even though my wrists were tied, my hands still had considerable movement.

What was I going to do? I could grab it and shoot him. I could grab the gun and threaten him, just as he had been doing to me.

To do any of these I needed to be able to move freely. However, I was somewhat restricted by the chains around my wrists. There were also a couple of significant unknowns when it came to doing anything with this gun. One, I didn't know how to handle or fire such a weapon. Was there a safety catch and if so where was it and how would I turn off such a catch? Two, was the gun loaded?

Then there was the complicated issue of me being the teacher and the children witnessing me shooting someone. What sort of behaviour should I be presenting? What if there was a struggle and the gun went off and one of the children was shot? What then?

All these thoughts ran through my mind within a split second.

I opted not to grab the gun.

After the event, this scenario was the one thing that repeatedly played over in my mind more than any other, causing me to have 'palpitating episodes'. Whenever I thought about what might have been and how close I had come to grabbing that gun and either shooting him or threatening him, my heart raced uncontrollably, adrenalin would pump through my body, I'd have a sudden urge to go to the toilet, my face would go as red as a beetroot and I would feel hot all over.

What if I had shot him in front of the children? What effect would that have had on them?

What if I had shot and killed him? How would I have felt? How would I have lived with the sense of guilt?

What if there had been a struggle causing the gun to go off and one of the children was injured or worse still, killed? What would have happened then? Where would I have been today?

What if…? The scenarios that played out in my mind for years afterwards always ended badly.

To this day, I am so glad I didn't touch that gun!

After securing Kay and Leanne, the gunman was facing the back of the room and was starting to chain up Jill.

Dale remained in his position closest to the door. Along with the rest of the children he was not yet shackled. Still free! He was sitting expectantly in his seat eyeing the proceedings with a quizzical look on his face. The gunman was still facing the back of the room. Dale and I were not in his line of sight.

To execute my escape plan, I made eye contact with Dale.

'Go!' I mouthed, accompanied by a slight hand gesture and movement of my head. 'Go!'

Dale was still by the door and being a local, living only about four hundred metres from the school, this seemed like a reasonable idea to me. Certainly, the best of any I'd been able to come up with so far. Dale was only six years old, but he knew the area and the road between his place and the school like the back of his hand. His aunt and uncle lived even closer, about half way between his house and the school. I was hoping that we may have been able to get one of these neighbour's help and I thought Dale might be the link.

Again, I exaggeratedly mouthed the word, 'Go!' with a thrust of my head, with raised eyebrows and eyes opened as wide as possible. Dale just looked at me. With a mystified look on his face, he in turn mouthed back to me, 'What? What do you want?'

At this point, the gunman seemed to realise there was some extra activity going on behind him. He turned in my direction and threatened, 'Don't you try anything smart Teach, or I'll blow your head off.' I nodded and looked resignedly at Dale and all the children.

Again, after the event, this little cameo also played out in my mind repeatedly. What would have happened if Dale had tried to sneak out of the room? What trauma would Dale have gone through if he had been able to do what I wanted and run home, or to his aunt's and uncle's place? His sense of panic about the situation and fear of the gunman shooting him while running away to alert his family would have traumatised him unnecessarily. What would have happened if he had been able to get out the door, started to run for home and then the gunman had seen him and chased after him? Would he have taken a shot?

It makes me cringe to think about it.

My escape plan had the potential to be a life saver, but it also had the potential to have brought about death and trauma. I'm so thankful that Dale had no idea what I was on about.

I decided I wouldn't try a risk like that again and place the children in further jeopardy. We proceeded to do exactly what we were told. For the sake of the children I needed to play this right.

Look unperturbed.

Keep calm.

Act as if everything is fine.

I tried my best to continue with the unruffled look. It must have been reasonably effective because Bernie, a particularly bright and creative grade four student, made a very interesting statement to reporters after the ordeal. When she was asked what Mr. Hunter's response to the masked gunman's intrusion and demands was, she described my reaction as, 'He just thought it was a joke.'

Little did she and the rest of the students know that I was like a lot of teachers in demanding situations — behaving like a duck, staying calm on the surface but paddling like mad under the water.

However, this wasn't just a demanding situation, this was an invasion!

One at a time, each of the children's left hands were firmly fastened to the chain.

Bernie, with amazing insight, asked the gunman, 'Have you done this sort of thing before?'

'No. I haven't,' he answered.

It was to be sometime later that I found out that his answer was a lie... and what a big lie it was!

Helplessly, I watched as each child was secured. The children had their own individual reactions. Maggie and Jill, both in grade six, were two of the eldest. They in particular looked worried. There was serious puzzlement in Maggie's eyes. Jill was staring in bewilderment at the intruder. Their maturity, along with that of Lucy, also in grade six, and Leanne in grade five, meant they understood how serious the implications were of being tied up by a masked man. Lucy, whose bright, cheery smile always brightened up the classroom, was downcast. Her face was ashen. Leanne, who would normally have had the happiest of faces, looked troubled. She had a deep frown on her face, not sure of what was happening. Leanne was an eldest child and took on a lot of responsibility for her younger siblings. This was usually done conscientiously, accompanied with bright, nervous little mannerisms. Each of these older girls were anxious for everyone's welfare. Glances at me. Fearful looks at the gunman. Fleeting glimpses at the other children. Stares down at their own wrists securely padlocked to a sparkly new dog chain.

Ron was also in grade five. He was a very diligent but an affable and well-liked student. He had an enquiring look on his face but wasn't showing the same degree of anxiety as the girls.

The two children in the middle grades weren't showing the serious concern of the older ones either, but I could see their uneasy expressions. Bernie was in grade four. She was looking inquisitively at the gunman. Kay, in grade three, didn't seem overly concerned, but had a curious look about her.

The two youngest were both in grade two. Dale, near the door, and Russell, next to me, seemed mostly unworried by the tying up process. They only appeared to have questioning looks on their faces as they watched each of the older ones being secured.

Once everyone was fastened together the gunman ordered us to the door. We were all tied up in one long line. Dale at the beginning, me at the end. With the jingle of metal, we stood up, each of us joined by hand to the chain and dodging tables and desks, we worked our way across the room in the direction of the door like a disorganised chain gang.

The gunman followed us.

The chain gang of ten was the teacher and his nine pupils. This was not what a rural school was supposed to look like.

A 'rural school' was considered a school with just one or two teachers and up to thirty children. Rural schools have a totally unique character. They have a strong family atmosphere with the older children often taking special care of the younger. These schools are usually made up of multiple children from the same family — brothers and sisters, cousins and more distant relatives as well. Everyone knows everything about everyone else. The school is sometimes the only joint establishment for the local community and in Wooreen this was certainly the case. The Wooreen community had no local church or hall, no local fire brigade, sporting club or any other joint community body or building. The school was the heart of the community.

Right now though, a complete anomaly was taking place at this rural school.

Chained together, we were assembling on the orders of a masked gunman in the entry area. This area involved two doors very close together, the classroom door and the outside door. The classroom door opened into the entry room, which also served as the office, kitchen and storeroom. There were storage shelves, cupboards, a sink, filing cabinet, office equipment and the telephone. The telephone in particular was on my mind.

All ten of us were now standing in that entry area. Dale, Ron and Bernie had moved through into the entry room. The rest of the children were standing in the doorway and back in the classroom with Russell and me.

The gunman began to make his way past the children into the entry room. As he moved past the children, I walked up onto the platform and to the front right corner of the classroom. Russell followed. I was out of view of the gunman. His red bag was there, along with a variety of contents that had fallen out onto the floor. The bag, best described as a canvas kit bag, was about sixty centimetres long and thirty centimetres deep, although it was considerably flatter resting on the floor. Inside were papers of some sort, more padlocks and keys. A length of rope spilled onto the floor. A rough piece of cardboard had fallen out of the bag and was now resting on the floor. It looked like it had been torn off the edge of a cardboard box. It was rectangular, about twenty centimetres by fifteen centimetres. Written on it immaculately in red Texta, all in capital letters, were the words:

**HAVE GONE ON A NATURE
STUDY TRIP, WILL BE BACK
IN ONE HOUR!**

I deduced that the gunman intended to display it somewhere, to mislead the parents and anyone else who visited the school and to suggest that I had taken the children for a Nature Study Trip. This annoyed me. He had written a notice, making out that it was me who had written it. It startled me. It made me angry. How dare he?

Despite the crazy circumstances, I was also irritated by the way it was written. His use of capital letters was wrong. Any primary teacher worth his weight uses every opportunity to model and teach the use of correct upper and lower-case letters. I would not have written that note in capital letters. Nor would I have used a scrappy piece of cardboard. Schools, of all places, have ample paper to write on.

In hindsight it was silly of me to be concerned about such matters. However, I hoped that observers would be astute enough to recognise that it was not my work and would realise that we had been taken away against our wills.

I also recognised that it was a shrewd move on the gunman's part. It was becoming more obvious to me that he was well prepared in what he was doing and we were in serious trouble.

Despite the lettering and dodgy piece of cardboard, the notice ensured that if any parents or other person came visiting the school during school hours, the absence of the teacher and children was easily explained. This bought the gunman precious time, as who would know when the 'hour' began? Alarm bells wouldn't start ringing until at least an hour after the visitor arrived. And it would look as if I was the person who had taken the children away.

I had a strong sense that I was in an awful predicament, along with the children in my care. I was responsible for these children. Their parents had entrusted them to me. What were the parents going to think? How were they going to react when they turned up at school to find a notice with some 'cock and bull' story about being out for a nature study trip, only to discover we had disappeared to who knew where?

Flaming hell!

As the gunman was moving past us, he explained that he had to retrieve his car from the back road and that we were to wait, standing at the front door ready for a quick getaway. His car was parked on the back road at the south end of the school ground, about seventy-five metres from the school building, for fear of being seen by passersby.

This might give us time to make a phone call or provide the opportunity to make a run for it.

The phone was sitting on the filing cabinet in the office, where he and some of the children were now standing.

My other hope was that someone would drop in right there and then. A parent bringing a forgotten lunch or a mum picking up a child for an appointment, a visiting teacher or a travelling salesman wanting to sell some new educational supplies.

The school building could be plainly seen by passing cars. The building was little more than fifteen metres east of the Leongatha-Yarragon Road. There were only a few small shrubs obscuring the building from various angles. I hoped that someone would see us or come from that direction. Making a run for it was a possibility, although being chained together would make running very awkward. There were limited places to run to as well. The only other structures on site were the toilet block, a storage shed and some basic playground equipment to the north and east sides of the main building. The closest neighbours were Dale's and Bernie's relatives to the north. I wondered if we might be able to run in that direction. The other direction was towards the back road at the south of the school, where the gunman had parked his vehicle. It was a gravel road to Mirboo North — the same road that I had travelled on that morning on my way to school. We wouldn't be running in that direction since that was where he was about to go.

The gunman was preparing to go and pick up his vehicle. Up to this point he had kept his balaclava over his head, hiding the upper part of his face. Before going back outside the school, he removed the mask. He had a long straight crop of very dark, near black hair. He wore a thick black moustache. The rest of his face was unshaven, with at least a week's growth of very dark stubble. He had brown eyes with thick, dark eyebrows. He looked about thirty years of age.

Even though he looked like a far more 'regular' guy with his mask off, I was still alarmed by the situation.

To my great disappointment, but not unsurprisingly, he dealt with the phone before walking outside. We all watched as he unscrewed the cover of the ear piece and ripped the inside wiring and speaker out of its resting place and put it in his pocket.

He said, 'I don't want to wreck the phone but it's necessary. You'll have to get a new one.'

He then screwed the ear piece cover back in place. To look at, the phone appeared untouched.

That's one way to deal with a phone. So much for that avenue of help.

Before leaving the building, the gunman walked past all the children and back into the classroom where I was standing and said, 'I still don't trust you, Teach. I'm going to make sure you can't try to run off on me.' He then padlocked my end of the chain to one of the coat hangers right next to me, on which the children hung their bags. The hanger was about one metre off the floor. It was a sturdy structure and able to support a heavy weight. There was no way I would have been able to yank it off the wall. This was just inside the classroom door. There were fewer than fifty centimetres between my hands and the end of the chain, now secured to the wall. I had very little room for movement.

He then ordered us to sit down. We obeyed.

Unable to use my hands for support, since they were attached so closely by chain to the hanger, I bent down and knelt on the floor. My hands became slightly elevated as I moved into a sitting position.

Once again, the gunman reminded me not to try anything smart.

'No notes or messages written anywhere Teach. Don't you try to be a hero pal. I'll be checking.'

He opened the outside door, walked out into the open air, firmly closing the door behind him and I guessed that he started heading for his vehicle.

My mind raced. What could I do? There didn't look to be any avenue of manoeuvre. The gunman appeared to have every base covered. Except for an unexpected visitor or a sovereign act of God, there was nothing that could be done, so it seemed.

I didn't want to be a hero, nor did I see any opportunity to do anything that might seem in the slightest bit heroic. Hadn't the intruder just warned me not to be a hero? So far, any possible avenue of escape or seeking help had drawn blanks. Hero or not I had to do something. I had to stop this!

I thought that if I could get all the children outside, chained together and wave like mad, that a passer-by might see us and think something was awry. I instructed the children to stand up and move through the door. I wanted as many of them to stand outside the door as possible, as far as the chain could stretch. Despite my end of the chain being fastened to the coat hanger just inside the classroom, most of the children would be able to reach outside, I thought.

With my nerves on high alert and my insides still shaking, I tried to speak as calmly and firmly as possible.

'Everyone, stand up,' I said. 'Dale, open the door and lead the way outside and everyone follow. We want people to see us. They might stop and help.'

I quickly explained to them that they should all wave like mad at anyone passing by, so that we could alert them to our predicament.

One of the older children was not happy about this.

'Mr. Hunter! Please. No! He'll come back and he'll shoot us. Please. No!'

The rest of the children seemed to follow the older child's lead and there was an immediate general consensus that they thought my idea was not worth the risk.

Not wanting to stress the children more than necessary and very aware that it was only a long shot, I reluctantly said, 'Okay, we'll just wait here.' I recognised that although cars passed by fairly regularly, like every five to ten minutes, the chances of one passing in those moments before the gunman came back were very low. And the chances of the passing motorist seeing our waving and realising the seriousness of our predicament was even more remote.

Look unperturbed.

Keep calm.

Act as if everything is fine.

Just then, having only been gone no more than a minute, he was back. He opened the door, looked inside and with a funny look on his face said, 'I thought I had forgotten something, but I mustn't have.' Then he went outside again. Tricky. I guessed that he was making sure that we weren't up to something or perhaps he wanted to keep us guessing.

So, what could I do? Something, surely! I couldn't write a note as he said he would be checking. So that seemed like folly. My hands were tied in more ways than one. The children didn't want to move. I felt like I was stuck in a corner with no place to go.

The classroom electric clock hung high on the wall above my head. The cord was plugged in to my right, just out of reach. Although I couldn't reach it, I mentally noted that unplugging it would be a good idea, that it would indicate what time of the day we'd been taken away. The plug didn't have an on/off switch. To stop the clock, it was necessary to unplug it from the socket.

The children and I heard a vehicle start up at the south end of the school, enter the school ground, turn around and then back up close to the front door.

I glimpsed the vehicle through the western side window. It was a grey Dodge utility truck, very similar to the vehicles that I had seen the State Electricity Commission workers using. It had a square cabin at the rear, separated from the front cabin. Small windows lined the sides of the rear cabin and there was a window into the front compartment. The rear cabin doors opened up and down.

After getting out of the utility, we could hear the man open the back doors. He then hurriedly opened the school door, stepped inside and in a rush said, 'I've changed my mind about you, Teach.'

Thoughts raced through my mind.

What was he going to do with me?

Leave me behind and simply take the children alone?

Shoot me?

Was I ready to die?

Death certainly seemed to be on the cards at this point. Over my short life I had thought about the certainty of death. One of my aunts had recently died and I had experienced the death of both of my grandmothers. One of my best mates had lost both his parents while we'd been in our later years of high school. But was I ready to die at the hand of a crazed gunman? In front of my school children? Perhaps slowly and painfully?

Heaven forbid!

Please Lord!

Not like that.

He moved into the classroom towards me, fumbling in his left pocket for something. His gun was in his front right pocket.

He stated, 'The first thing I have to do is unlock this chain from the wall.'

He sorted through a number of keys until he found the right one and then inserted the key into the lock right next to me.

He was very close. I could smell him. It was obvious that he had been living rough for some time. His body odour was bad. His unshaven and unkempt appearance was right before me. I could also smell stale breath and cigarettes.

He was trying to undo the lock. It wasn't working for him.

He complained, 'So who's been tampering with the lock?'

What a lot of rubbish. You can't undo the lock, so you're blaming us?

The children all looked rather bewildered at this accusation as if to say, 'What? Not me!'

It made me think that we should have tampered with the lock, by shoving some small objects in the key hole while he was away, so that he couldn't have undone the lock easily. At least he would have been slowed down whilst attempting to undo the lock, increasing our chances of someone coming to our rescue.

All of a sudden, the lock was undone.

He said, 'That's right. You have to turn the key.'

Comedian.

He then started moving back through the door, past the children. Being freed from the wall I moved towards the front of the room with Russell close behind me. Ted stopped and looked directly at me.

What is this change of mind he said he had? Is that what he's about to do?

'Pass me my bag please, Teach.'

The politeness of his request was both surprising and confusing.

He was just inside the outer doorway. I was still in the classroom, not very far from his bag which was near the blackboard. Some of the children stood chained between us. I wondered why he wanted me, with chained hands, to pass him his bag when he could have come back around to get it himself. I gauged that he was in a hurry and that the children were partly blocking him from getting back into the room.

I bent over and picked up his bag with my two shackled hands.

The rope was next to the bag. It was white, approximately six millimetres thick and three metres long. Then there was the cardboard notice which he was presumably planning on displaying somewhere. With my foot, I subtly moved the notice away from sight further into the corner near a gap between the wall and a cupboard, hoping that it would be a case of, 'out of sight, out of mind'. I then lifted the bag over the children. He reached out over the children from near the doorway and took the bag.

With the bag now in his hand, the gunman moved through the inner doorway, bent over and walked under some of the children's chained up arms and moved back into the main part of the school room.

He then asked me to pass him the rope. Again, I bent down and with chained hands, grasped the rope and passed it to him.

By this stage he had come back into the classroom and was right next to me. I was in the corner of the room standing on the small platform with the cardboard notice partly obscured on the floor behind me.

Before I found out my fate, he asked me to pass him the bit of cardboard.

Damn. Nice try.

I passed him the scrap of cardboard. He took a hammer that was tucked away in his bag and then moving back out into the open-air he began nailing the notice to the outside door.

Then I remembered the clock.

While he was hammering the notice, I quickly moved back to where the clock was plugged in. I reached down and unplugged the electric plug from the socket, thus stopping the clock. It read 11.10am.

Later, when the police arrived, with the clock still displaying 11.10am, along with all the other pieces of evidence, it helped them ascertain that we had been kidnapped by an intruder, since they could deduce the time that we had been taken from the school.

The gunman quickly came back inside. Not wasting a minute, he ordered me once again to lie down on the floor. Was this when he was going to shoot me?

'Lie face down. Put your arms up above your head. Don't try anything smart.'

With a key he unlocked my padlock, unwound the chain from around my wrists, freeing me from my constraints. Despite the fear, it was nice to have my hands and wrists free again. I felt light. He then took a step back and stared at me. He had his hand on the butt of his gun which was in his front right pocket. He just stood there looking at me. The children stood, chained behind me and out of my view, but I knew they would be watching the proceedings closely.

Please God, no.

I really thought that might have been it: that he was going to shoot me.

Without saying a word, however, the gunman focused his attention on the rope and prepared to secure me for a second time. He asked me to sit up and put my hands behind my back. He tied my wrists tightly together and wound the rope firmly around my waist, pinning my arms in hard against my back. The rope was then knotted at my front.

I'd played games as a child where my older brothers would tie me up with hay band and see how long it would take me to untie myself. It was fun because it had never taken long. Ted's securing seemed to be on a different level to those games. I wasn't getting out of this in a hurry.

It seemed like my life was being extended, at least for the short term. Being tied up was better than being shot.

The gunman had brought some masking tape back from his vehicle. He quickly peeled back a fifteen-centimetre strip and cut the strip off with some scissors. He then stuck it over my mouth while stating, 'Sorry about this, Teach, but I can't afford for you to be a smart ass.'

Working quickly, he peeled off another considerably longer piece, cut it with his scissors and placed it over my eyes with the comment, 'Speak no evil. See no evil.'

Fair enough. Witty.

Does that mean I am going or staying?

Dead or alive?

Tied up. Blinded. Gagged. Not sure if I was about to be shot. My students all tied up. An armed man making demands. This was not how teaching was supposed to be. How was I going to look after the children? I wanted to reassure them that everything would be okay, but was it all okay? I knew I needed to be taking care of them. I felt for the poor kids. Chained up and being taken off to some unknown destination. And having to watch their teacher tied up, sworn at, threatened, blindfolded, gagged and helplessly overpowered. This was not right.

I was in darkness, with the tape over my eyes. I knew there was light but I couldn't see it. I couldn't see my students. I couldn't see my captor. I felt completely vulnerable. Thankfully I could still hear. I listened like I had never listened before. I heard the movement and voices of the children, the steps of the gunman, the jingle of chains; link clinking against link, the chain dragging on the floor. They were all in the doorway and entry area, preparing to exit the building.

I needed help but there was none to be had. Where were all my friends and family when I needed them? Throughout my life I'd had all the support and love and care that anyone could have wished for. Where were they now? I had a strong sense of isolation, being alone and cut off from all supports.

>>><<<

I'd had a privileged upbringing. My parents were steady, hard-working people who had loved me and brought me up with as much care and support as possible. I had four older brothers. Frank, my eldest brother by fourteen years was like a second father to me. Along with my other three brothers he had encouraged and supported me, and I'd always looked up to each of them, like idols.

Neville, my second eldest brother was a school teacher and was one of the main reasons why I was in this job. I was following his lead. I had loved visiting him at his various schools, two of them being rural schools, where he had been the Headmaster, like I now was. Neville and his wife had even gone out of their way on their recent January holidays to have a look at Wooreen and the district, in the knowledge of my appointment at the school.

My brother Chris and I were very close, partly because we were closest in age. These three of my four older brothers were all married. Each of their wives had fully embraced me as their little brother. Likewise, Ian, my second closest brother in age, had always shown particular interest in my life. He wasn't married but had started paying special attention to a girl who I'd gone through high school and teacher's college with.

I had also been blessed with quality friends that were loyal, kind and who would do anything for me; but right now, they were not to be found. I felt very much alone.

I missed all the tiny details of my family and friends acutely.

>>><<<

In my dark state I continued to listen. The children, very wisely, knowing that they were about to be taken away from school, asked if they could take their lunches and drink bottles with them. Mercifully, the gunman obliged. Their bags were in the entry way, where most of them were now standing, so it wasn't too difficult for them to grab their supplies, even with the limitations of one hand partly immobilised.

Well done kids! I thought from my blinded and dumb state. *Good thinking.* It hadn't been something that was on my mind. Far from it.

Most of the play lunches — that is, their snacks from recess, including Dale's apple — remained on the desks.

Concerned about being seen by passersby, the gunman ordered everyone to be quiet and stand still, so he could first listen to make sure there were no vehicles approaching. He then opened the door and hustled the children, all chained together, into the back of his vehicle. The noise of the chain dragging on the ground and then scraping against the tail gate panels of the utility as the children scrambled up and into the back was a loud grating and rattling. I heard him telling them to lie down in such a way so they couldn't be seen. I wondered how nine children chained together could all lie down and still fit into the back of the utility.

He left me alone in the classroom unable to do anything much, other than to listen and to think. I mused that if he was to shoot me, it was best to do it without the children watching. Although, I had a hunch that he wasn't going to shoot me right then, since he'd gone to the trouble of tying me up so thoroughly.

I heard him talking with the children, telling them he had stolen a supply of milk for them to drink and they could help themselves. I heard him slam the back doors of the utility and his footsteps coming back inside through the two doorways and towards me.

I waited with fearful anticipation.

He said, 'Okay, Teach. Up you get. You're going in the front with me.'

Aah! What a relief. I'm going too. Thank you, God.

Hurriedly, he guided me out of the classroom, through the entry way, out of the school into the open air and to the passenger door of the utility. Unable to see my footing I walked hesitantly, being pulled along by the arm.

He said, 'Quick. Get in. Watch your head.'

I climbed in with difficulty, feeling my way. With my bottom first, I wriggled up onto the seat with my legs and feet following. He closed the door behind me.

The cabin was hot and smelt of cigarette smoke. I could also smell dust and sweat. I heard him go back into the school, presumably to get his things and check that everything was in order. I wondered if he might see the clock unplugged. I thought about my car parked behind the school and the fact that my wallet, watch and keys were still on my desk. Would he worry about such detail?

I heard the school door slam shut, him briskly approaching and then passing the right-hand rear of the vehicle. He yelled at the children, all crammed in the back cabin, 'You kids keep down. When we're passing any cars, keep your heads right down or bullets will be flying.'

Man. Oh man! You mongrel! They're my students you're yelling at.

How dare you threaten them like that!

He then very quickly opened the driver's side door, shoved something between him and myself, which I assumed was his bag, and climbed into his seat.

I must have looked a sight, sitting up in full view in the passenger's seat, with strips of masking tape over my eyes and mouth. Not the sight that he would have wanted anyone to witness as he drove out of the school.

His first words were, 'Get down off the seat. Get on the floor. I can't have you sitting up there.'

Okay. You had better move Robert.

This meant turning my body around and sliding down from the seat until my knees rested on the floor. Not being able to see and not having my hands or arms free to support my weight made it quite a difficult manoeuvre. I found myself uncomfortably kneeling on the floor with my stomach and chest resting on the seat to gain some sort of balance. The hot vinyl seat pressed against my body through my shirt. I could feel the heat on my face and smell the hot vinyl.

'Whenever we pass a car you better keep your head right down or it will roll,' the gunman ordered.

Man! You don't want much!

I was still hoping that someone would see what was happening. But with the children's and my heads being forced to stay down it was becoming less of a possibility.

He was preparing to drive off. I estimated the time to be 11.20am.

I could hardly move. I couldn't see. My only supports were my knees on the floor and my chest on the seat. I tried to brace myself with my feet against the sides of the floor, up against the door with my right foot and the hump along the centre of the chassis with my left foot, in readiness for the drive.

I wondered how the children were going to fare. I felt so cut off from them. What if they needed the toilet? What if they were car sick or injured in the back, who would be caring for them then? I was supposed to be ensuring their health and safety. I wondered how crammed and uncomfortable they were, all chained together, lying down. Thankfully, I thought, the older children would be looking after the younger, making sure they were okay, giving instructions and helping them where needed. So far, they had all seemed to be holding up well.

Under the best of circumstances, teachers are sometimes most aptly nicknamed 'control freaks.' Although I'd only been teaching eight and a-quarter days for my whole career, I know I still came under that category. The need for control in a classroom of children is obvious. However, the disarray, noise, disrespect and general chaos that can sometimes occur in a classroom is a nightmare and something that most teachers have experienced. Teachers often come to fear such chaos, which is why we transform into control freaks more generally. This was certainly the case for me. I'd experienced a series of classroom situations throughout my teacher training where I was constantly on edge, feeling like the class was nearly out of control. I wanted to avoid this feeling at all costs. As a result, I had made sure that I was always fully prepared and ready for any scenario.

Any scenario? Not possible. Not today. I was certainly not in control at this point.

I was deeply worried. 'Oh God!' I prayed, 'What am I to do? Please look after us.'

I abandoned myself to God's care and to the mercies of this 'nutter'.

ON THE ROAD: 11.20AM

Off he drove at a very rapid rate, out the front gate, turning right, heading north and then veering around a bend, off the bitumen onto a gravel road, in a general north-easterly direction. The gunman left our little Wooreen State School, Victorian School No. 3723, far behind.

Wooreen, two hundred kilometres south-east of Melbourne, is located between the steep, rugged peaks of the Strzelecki Ranges to the north and the gentle, rolling hills of Leongatha to the south. It was towards the Strzeleckis that we were now headed.

The children had a good grasp of where we were travelling since they knew the area so well and were able to see through the windows above their heads. I later found out that Dale was particularly aware of the route, as it took us right past his house. Taking a risk, he'd lifted his head slightly and noticed his mother out the front of their house mowing the lawn.

After the first few turns I became completely disoriented. I had no idea in which direction we were travelling.

Although I did not know this at the time, we veered off the main Leongatha-Yarragon Road and followed Forresters Road until we reached the Grand Ridge Road, where we turned right. This road follows some of the highest parts of the Strzelecki Ranges, the highest mountains in South Gippsland. Except for a short distance through Mirboo North, this was an entirely unsealed gravel road.

Despite the conditions, the gunman drove like a madman. We raced and skidded around corners, bouncing up and down on the unsealed, bumpy and rough roads. I was incredibly uncomfortable in my kneeling position. The smell of dust was acute. It was up my nose and very soon had filled the whole cabin. The children were being pushed and catapulted around in the back of the vehicle: I could hear them being buffeted about, thrown against the walls and floor of the vehicle as we hit the bumps, the pot holes and corners. There were regular exclamations of pain from the impact. They too would be getting covered in dust. Breathing it in, filling their nostrils.

Fair go mate. Slow down! The kids are going to get hurt.

Even if I had been able to speak I probably wouldn't have had the guts to utter such words. What do you say to the man who holds the gun? Assertiveness was not one of my strong points at the best of times. I had always been very willing to throw my weight around aggressively on the football field and as a teacher, I was able to deliver instructions with a certain amount of confidence, however, when it came to asserting myself with other adults, I would have to describe myself as a bit of a chicken.

This scenario came into a whole new category. I wasn't sure what lengths I was prepared to go, but I knew if the need arose, I would put my life on the line for the sake of the children.

>>><<<

I was twenty years old and I was extremely green. I had completed three years of intense teacher training at the Bendigo College of Advanced Education. It was excellent preparation and as good as any that the Victorian teacher training institutions offered at that time. But I was young, inexperienced and naive. I just didn't realise to what extent, at the time.

I had arrived at the school a week before the starting date to meet the School Council President, to be given the keys and a brief orientation to the buildings and surrounds. I'm very aware now that I would have appeared so ill equipped to take on such a role as Headmaster of my own school. The School Council President must have scratched his head with wonder at how such a young, long haired, untidy character could possibly teach his children and the rest of the students in the school.

My appearance was somewhat typical of the 1970s. My hair was well overdue for a cut, dark brown and curly. I was six-foot-tall with a lean build. I had grown a beard in an attempt to hide my youthfulness, in the hope of gaining more respect from the children. The beard was totally unkempt. It was ginger in colour, thick and bushy, certainly not fitting to my aspirations of being respected as a professional. It made me look more like a Ned Kelly type bushranger than an educator. Why hadn't somebody told me how ridiculous I looked? I don't remember if they had. I don't remember anyone preparing me in any way for this drama either.

>>><<<

As the gunman continued to drive in a very dangerous manner, I tried to brace myself in any way I was able. The children in the back continued to be bounced around and thrust from side to side.

One of the children called out, 'Slow down!' I thought it was Lucy.

The gunman ignored the lone voice of reason.

I felt more helpless than I had ever felt in my life. Choosing to become the Headmaster of a Rural School had been a significant risk on my part. I knew it would be a hard job, but this situation was out of the blue. Although I knew I was to be on my own at the school, I had a number of supports available to me. My District Inspector (the Education Department's head of that region) Ray Bull and my supervising Principal Pat Higgins at Leongatha Primary School had been in contact with me before school started, congratulating me on my appointment and offering their support for anything I needed. Their support was needed right now!

I also had a Rural School Consultant who was to visit me from time to time and my Group Leader at Hallston Primary School, ten kilometres further up the road, who I could call on for help. We were scheduled to have a Group Day once or twice a term at Hallston, involving the three or four schools within a fifteen-kilometre radius. It didn't seem like they were going to be any help at this moment either. It was in the general direction of Hallston that we were now headed, not for the scheduled Group Day, but at the hands of a crazed gunman.

We continued swerving left and right, hard and sharp, a couple of times almost stopping and then turning in different directions.

I had always prided myself in having a strong sense of direction. Around my home town, the roads all went in orthodox north-south and east-west directions, so I always knew where I was heading.

Having been brought up on a farm I understood directions. As well as the east west movement of the sun, I knew the directions that the different types of weather came from. I have vivid memories of helping Dad repair the western weather boards on our house and Dad's explanations to me of the impact of the sun on the west side of the house on a summer's day. 'Merciless.' These bearings had become a part of me.

But up to this point I had not driven more than a kilometre north from the school, at any stage. I had always come from the south and easterly directions on entirely different and much more direct routes. Although I knew that we were initially heading in the direction of Hallston, which I'd never been near, I was now totally clueless as to where we were and what direction we were heading.

And so right now, tearing around bends left and right, facing the wrong way and not able to see, all sense of direction was lost.

The gunman talked to me. Unable to answer, I just listened. He made some comment about me behaving very well. He suggested that my passive approach was wise.

Thanks a lot. Encouragement from a nutcase.

Something about his words didn't sit right with me.

'You'll want to thank me for this one day,' he continued, 'Yes, you'll become famous. Everyone will want to know you and know the story.'

I had no understanding or idea of the possibilities of such talk.

Wanting some response, he leaned over and yanked the masking tape off my mouth. I lost a considerable amount of beard in that moment and it didn't tickle!

Talking to my crazed captor in my blind and helpless state was not on my list of priorities at that moment.

He asked me what my name was.

'Rob,' I answered.

He told me he'd been planning this procedure for some time and that I was the lucky one.

I didn't respond.

Lucky one? I don't think so!

>>><<<

I'd decided that I wanted to be a teacher at the age of fifteen. A number of factors influenced this.

Firstly, there was no room to work on our family dairy farm in Northern Victoria, Kyabram, as three of my older brothers had laid claim to that avenue of employment.

Secondly, Dad encouraged me to pursue higher education with words such as, 'Rob, you've got a good brain,' and 'I can see you being a teacher or in a similar profession that requires brains.' These words had a significant impact on me.

I'm not sure whether Dad really believed his encouragements or whether it simply suited the fact that there was no room left on the farm for the youngest of five sons. In retrospect, I don't think I had any more brains than any of the others. But thankfully, I took the endorsements to heart and set my sights on teaching or some other suitable profession.

Thirdly, my brother Neville was a primary teacher. His example helped pave the way for my decision.

Then also, as a Christian, I had decided that I wanted to have the maximum possible influence for good on society and I believed that teaching had the potential to be that positive influence, so becoming a teacher seemed like a good option.

The other factor that had an impact was a significant conversation that I had with one of my teachers early in form four.

Mr. Knight was his name. One day at lunch time we began chatting in the yard. He asked me questions. He listened to what I had to say. He seemed genuinely interested in my life and it gave me such a buzz. I wasn't expecting this conversation because Mr. Knight and I had a history. He'd been my class teacher in form three where our exchanges consisted of little more than him punishing me for talking while sitting at the back of the class. Yet on this occasion he conversed one on one with me for what seemed like an eternity. I was caught by surprise. I walked away from that conversation convinced that teaching was for me, knowing that teachers had the potential to have a massive effect on people's lives.

I completed my teacher training on a 'studentship,' which meant that I had joined the Education Department as an exit student at high school. I had the privilege of being paid to train as a teacher, on one condition: that I promised to work for at least two years with the Education Department. That didn't seem to be too much of an onerous task. It was exactly what I wanted and seemed just right for me.

However, would I still be alive to fulfil that two-year agreement?

>><<<

My immediate problem however, was of a slightly different kind. Travelling so fast around corners, bouncing up and down, and facing the wrong direction while blindfolded meant that I soon felt rather car sick. Thankfully, the gag was now off my mouth, so the impending vomit was at least able to be expelled. The resultant puke went all over me and the seat. This continued for some time. I retched until I could retch no more.

I felt like death.

The gunman enquired, 'Are you okay?'

'I'm okay,' I answered between heaves, even though I was far from okay.

He responded with a platitude. 'I know how you feel. I've been car sick before too and the "Stiffs" couldn't have cared less.'

Thanks!

The end result was vomit everywhere, all over the seat and down the sides, all over the front of my shirt and on parts of my trousers.

He leant across me and wound down the window. I felt the breeze cooling my clammy head. It was also slightly refreshing to breathe in some clean air instead of the putrid smell that was now filling my nostrils. I guess the gunman felt a similar relief. With a towel or rag that he produced from somewhere he reached out and briefly wiped my face, the front of my shirt and the seat.

Although only a fleeting thought, I appreciated his act of kindness.

With no option to rinse my mouth with water, the after-taste of vomit lingered. The acidic burning in my throat was extremely unpleasant. Despite the fresh air coming through the window the stench of vomit was intense.

The gunman asked me whether I thought he would receive a good ransom for the kids and me.

'Do you think I might get $40,000 out of the government?'

The question didn't seem to require an answer and was soon followed by the comment, 'I'm doing this so I can retire.'

Wow! He's going to the government to get money for us. That's no small ask. Retire? Sure thing! I doubt it mate. Criminals generally end up in jail.

In my present state, with the taste and smell of vomit still dominating my senses, I had little interest in ransoms. I wasn't even sure as to what a ransom actually was. My only familiarity with the term was that I'd heard of Jesus paying our ransom for our sins on the cross, but I hadn't fully understood the complete meaning of that either.

We drove for what I estimated to be about half an hour. I was still covered in vomit and dust with blindfold still in place, trussed like a Christmas turkey and listening to monologues and concepts that I didn't really understand.

And so the events of the Wooreen kidnapping of 1977 continued to unfold.

>>><<<

It's thirty-nine years ago now, as I put my fingers to the keys writing a formal account of those hours. Each of the people involved are so fresh in my mind. In some ways it's like yesterday. Even though there are gaps in my memory, the main events have been remembered, retold, pondered and reflected upon so often they have remained incredibly vivid and indelibly woven into my brain.

I had received my appointment to the school late the previous year. Having asked God to lead me in my decision of where to apply for my first appointment, I filled out the application form, electing 'Rural Schools' in 'South Gippsland' in the 'Leongatha area.' This process took place during the latter part of 1976, my last year of teacher training.

It seemed like a good idea at the time. The only thing I knew about the area was from a road trip I'd had with my parents through the South Gippsland hills years before. I remember being mesmerised by the beautiful green hills and attractive looking dairy farms. The fresh, green and undulating landscape was in vivid contrast to the dry, flat plains of my home area in Northern Victoria.

And then there was the girl that I had met a year or two before, who came from somewhere around Leongatha. The area might be just the place for me.

Having received my appointment in December 1976, I took on the adventure of driving all the way down to South Gippsland from my home town of Kyabram with my good mates Kevin and Peter.

Peter, like me, had just received his first appointment. He had been placed at Coalville, south of Moe in the Latrobe Valley, a well-known coal mining area. As the crow flies, our schools weren't more than thirty kilometres apart. But between us were the Strzelecki Ranges, with numerous peaks, many winding roads with precipitous drops and no direct route across. We visited Peter's school that day too. Kevin, like Peter and I, had just finished his teacher training at the Bendigo College of Advanced Education. Kevin had opted to pursue further study the following year at Monash University to ensure that he had a Bachelor of Education, a qualification that Peter and I would have to gain in the near future.

Kevin was excited for Peter's and my new appointments and was only too willing to join in the adventure of visiting the new schools. Peter and I planned to share a house together, so we also checked out Mirboo North as a possible place to

Wooreen State School 3723.

School ground.

Wooreen State School classroom.
Photos Courtesy Victoria Police Museum.

Chains and locks used in the kidnapping.

The gun used in the kidnapping.

Note left on the front door of the school.

*The stolen
Dodge utility.*

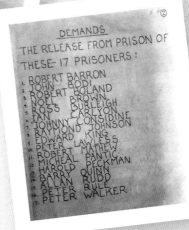

©

TO THE MINISTER OF EDUCATION
VIA THE EDITOR OF THE "SUNDAY-
OBSERVER";
GREETINGS MAGGOT!

ROUND 2

I HAVE KIDNAPPED THE TEACHER
AND PUPILS FROM THE ALLAMBEE WOOREEN
STATE PRIMARY SCHOOL.
IF MY DEMANDS AND CONDITIONS
ARE NOT ACCEDED TO, THE
HOSTAGES WILL BE KILLED.

*Ransom note pages
one and two of 10.*

②

DEMANDS
THE RELEASE FROM PRISON OF
THESE 17 PRISONERS:

1. ROBERT BARRON
2. JOHN BODI
3. ROBERT BOLAND
4. NOEL BROWN
5. ROSS BURLEIGH
6. IAN CARLYON
7. JOHNNY CONSIDINE
8. RAYMOND JOHNSON
9. EDWARD KING
10. PETER LAWLESS
11. ROBERT MATHEW
12. MICHEAL PANTIC
13. HAROLD PECKMAN
14. BARRY QUINN
15. ALLAN RUDD
16. PETER RULE
17. PETER WALKER

Envelope used for the ransom note.

Seat of Rob's trousers.

PANTS AND CUT OUT PIECE OF CLOTH SENT TO EDITOR SUNDAY OBSERVER WITH RANSOM NOTE

Robin Smith's logging truck.

TIMBER JINKER INVOLVED IN COLLISION DRIVER KIDNAPPED BY EASTWOOD

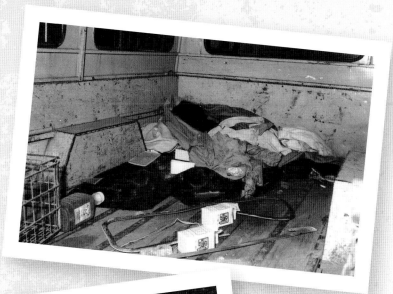

*Above: Inside of
the utility after the
accident.*

*Left: The mangled
utility near the
accident scene.*

The mangled utility.

Inside the utility after the accident.

*Shot out tyre of
the Kombi van.*

REAR TYRE SHOT BY POLICE

PROPERTY REMOVED FROM STORE
FOUND AT CAMPSITE

Stolen supplies.

Camp site in Mullungdung State Forest.

Kombi van belonging to Joy Edward.

Rescuers ready to start the search.

The rescuers being briefed.
Photos Courtesy Victoria Police Museum.

live, making some enquiries of places to rent. Mirboo North was about half way between our two schools. It ended up being where we made our home.

The weekend just gone had been a special one, where Kevin and quite a few other friends from teacher's college had come to stay with Peter and I at our new rental. They were all very interested to see our schools. On the Saturday afternoon we had driven all over the countryside, visiting both 'My Wooreen School' and 'Peter's Coalville School'. They were all engrossed in how we had set up our classrooms and what sort of lessons we were delivering and how we were juggling the multi-age groups. They were most encouraging and shared some ideas with us, which we were keen to try.

>>><<<

But now here I was the fully trained Bendigo College teacher, the Headmaster in charge of my own school with a predicament that I was totally unprepared for. My students' lives along with my own were in great danger at the hands of a madman.

THE LETTER: 11.45AM

We drove onto a sealed road. The even ride was a distinct contrast. Quieter and smoother. Not long after, we stopped.

The gunman called out to the children, 'Keep your heads down or watch out! If I see you waving to anyone I'll shoot someone!'

From my kneeling position beside the gunman I heard various movements. The opening and closing of the glove compartment, the rustle of papers accompanied by some incoherent utterances.

What is he doing? Writing something?

From the sounds of passing cars and even the sound of a distant voice I could tell that we were in some sort of built up area. A township of some type, I reasoned.

I wonder if we can get someone to see our plight.

Despite the gunman's threats I hoped that the children would make a scene and attract the attention of some passersby. I wondered if I might have been able to do something similar. I didn't know how I could possibly open the door, where the door handle was or whether the door was locked. I assumed the gunman had locked it. He had not mentioned the matter.

He asked me if I had my wallet on me or any other form of ID. I answered in the negative. He then explained to me that since I didn't have any ID, he needed to take some material from my trousers to place in a letter that he was going to post to the press demanding a ransom. He told me he was going to cut it out from the seat of my pants.

Are you for real? I thought. Out of the bum of my pants? Couldn't you just cut a piece from my leg? What sort of a stunt is this? Are you trying to humiliate me in front of my school children as well as taking us away against our wills?

I had little choice. Kneeling on the floor, blindfolded and with my hands tightly secured behind my back, I was totally at his mercy.

This was the ransom letter that was to be published in the press, some days later. The gunman was posting a letter to the newspaper *The Sunday Observer*. With some of my pants!

This put new light on what was taking place. This was where his twisted mind was leading him. A letter to the press; using the media to get his demands. The extent and the impact of what he was doing to the children and I was slowly emerging.

With a pair of scissors, he proceeded to cut out a small piece of material, about a seven-centimetre square, from the seat of my trousers. I now had a hole in my pants, right over my left buttock.

Terrific!

So, for the rest of the time, throughout this ordeal, in front of the children, I moved around with a hole in the seat of my pants. Charming! The ironic thing about that is, that in the light of the drama that was unfolding I hardly gave it another thought. Under normal circumstances I would have been highly embarrassed. My embarrassment right then was virtually non-existent.

Why he needed to include some of my trousers, or some form of ID, wasn't clear to me. Surely it was obvious that he was holding us captive without needing proof. Was a sample of my trousers really evidence that I was captive anyway?

Unbeknown to me at the time, this letter that he was preparing contained an unreasonable and unbelievable set of
demands. There were ten pages to it. And just like the note that
had been nailed to the door of the school, it was all written with
incredible neatness and exactness, with perfectly formed capital letters throughout, but this time with one repeated spelling
error.

It was set out and read exactly as follows:

P1
TO THE MINISTER OF EDUCATION
VIA THE EDITOR OF THE "SUNDAY-
OBSERVER";
GREETINGS MAGGOT!

ROUND 2
I HAVE KIDNAPPED THE TEACHER
AND PUPILS FROM THE WOOREEN
STATE PRIMARY SCHOOL.
IF MY DEMANDS AND CONDITIONS
ARE NOT ACCEDED TO, THE
HOSTAGES WILL BE KILLED.

P2
DEMANDS
A. THE RELEASE FROM PRISON OF
   THESE 17 PRISONERS:
   1. ROBERT BARRON
   2. JOHN BODI
   3. ROBERT BOLAND
   4. NOEL BROWN

5. ROSS BURLEIGH

6. IAN CARLYON

7. "JOHNNY" CONSIDINE

8. RAYMOND JOHNSON

9. EDWARD KING

10. PETER LAWLESS

11. ROBERT MATHEW

12. MICHEAL PANTIC

13. HAROLD PECKMAN

14. BARRY QUINN

15. ALLAN RUDD

16. PETER RULE

17. PETER WALKER

P3

B. 7 MILLION DOLLARS (U.S.A).

C. 100 KILOS OF PURE LATIN AMERICAN
   COCAINE.

D. 100 KILOS OF PURE HEROIN.

P4
CONDITIONS

1. THE PRISONERS TO BE
   RELEASED ARE TO BE GIVEN
   AN UNCONDITIONAL PARDON
   IN WRITING APON RELEASE.

2. THEY ARE TO BE RELEASED
   AT 0700 HOURS ON FRIDAY
   THE 18TH OF FEBRUARY 1977,
   NO EARLIER, NO LATER.

3. EACH PRISONER APON RELEASE
IS TO BE ISSUED WITH:
  A. 10,000 DOLLARS (AUST.)
     IN USED, UN-MARKED $20
     NOTES.

P5

  B. A LATE MODEL CAR WITH A
     FULL TANK OF PETROL.
  C. A 72 HOUR EXONERATION
     FROM ANY FORM OF INTER-
     -CEPTION.
4. IN THE CASE OF MR. BURLEIGH,
HE IS TO BE ISSUED WITH:
  A. A SUITABLE VEHICLE TO
     TRANSPORT THE AMERICAN
     CURRENCY AND NARCOTICS.
  B. AN FN FAL LIGHT AUTOMATIC
     RIFLE.

P6

  C. 5,000 ROUNDS OF PHOSPHUR-
     -OUS TIPPED 7.62MM NATO ROUNDS
  D. 10 SPARE MAGAZINES.
  E. A MODEL 29 SMITH AND
     WESSON REVOLVER (6 ½ INCH
     BARREL)
     5,000 REMINGTON CARTRIDGES
     INDEX NUMBER 7144.
     (NO C4 PLUGS THANKYOU)

5. THE PRISONERS TO BE FREED
   MUST NOT BE MAL-TREATED
   IN ANY MANNER.

P7

6. ANY PRISONER WISHING TO
   REJECT THIS FREE PARDON
   MUST CONVINCE MR. BURLEIGH
   THAT THE DECISION IS OF
   THE PERSON'S OWN VOLITION.
7. IN THE EVENT THAT A PRISONER
   REJECTS THEIR FREE PARDON
   MR. BURLEIGH HAS THE RIGHT
   TO ELECT A SUBSTITUTE.
8. THERE MUST BE NO SURVELL-
   -ANCE UNDERTAKEN APON ANY
   OF THESE MEN AFTER RELEASE.

P8

9. THERE MUST NOT BE ANY
   HIDDEN ELECTRONIC DEVICES.
10. THE AMERICAN CURRENCY
    IS TO BE IN $100 BILLS,
    USED AND UN MARKED.
11. THE NARCOTICS ARE TO BE
    PLACED IN CLEAN PLASTIC
    RUBBISH CONTAINERS.

MR. BURLEIGH IS TO BE GIVEN
COMPLETE CHARGE OF THE

AMERICAN CURRENCY AND
NARCOTICS.

P9

12. FINALLY, IF ANY OF THESE
    CONDITIONS ARE NOT
    FOLLOWED TO THE LETTER,
    MY REACTION WILL BE AS
    IF THE COMPLETE RANSOM
    DEMAND WERE REJECTED
    OUTRIGHT.
    THIS MUST GO TO THE NEWS
    MEDIA IN IT'S ENTIRETY
    AT LEAST 24 HOURS BEFORE
    THE DEADLINE.

P10

IN A WORLD FULL OF
DISTRACTIONS I AM
ONE PERSON WHO WOULD
GO TO ANY LENGTH AND
SINK TO ANY DEPTH TO
ACHIEVE SUCCESS ON A
MISSION AT HAND!
LACK OF TIME TO GATHER
THE RANSOM IS NO EXCUSE
IN THIS THE "ERA OF THE
F111".

With this letter in his hands, the gunman exited the vehicle after stating, 'Stay there Teach! Don't try anything stupid or you know what might happen. I'll only be a second.'

Escape or creating a scene didn't seem to be an option.

As promised, he was back in the utility very quickly.

Also, unbeknown to me, this stop to post the ransom letter had taken place in what was now my new home town. We had stopped at the Mirboo North Post Office, just metres from where I had only two or three weeks before made my home. Peter and I had rented a house in Couper Street, less than one hundred metres from the Post Office.

I had got to know this area quite well in the short time of living there. Opposite the Post Office, on the north side of the road, was a large vacant area, yet to be developed. Our house was on the other side of that vacant area. The area was largely deserted, with scraggly grass that was only cut occasionally. I had walked across the area from our house in Couper Street to the Post Office and shopping area on a number of occasions in those first weeks. Just the day before I had kicked a football with Peter and some friends on this rough and uneven surface. Presumably this quiet out-of-the-way spot, close to a post box, suited the gunman's thinking.

If I had known where we were, would it have given me the encouragement to have made more effort to escape? Would I have been able to find the door handle and somehow managed to fall or climb out onto the side of the road and cause a scene? Would anyone have seen me?

If I had been able to get out of the vehicle and stumble away, tied up, blindfolded and gagged, what would the gunman have done? Left me there? Shot me?

Of course, I couldn't abandon the children. It was no good me running away and leaving them behind. I was responsible for them, for their safety and for their care.

NEAR DEATH: 12.00 MIDDAY

Off we sped again. It was probably about midday. I took particular notice of the first turns and distances after posting the letter, thinking that the knowledge may have been important at a later stage. Very soon after taking off we took a right-hand turn and not long after a left-hand turn. We then braked heavily and drove relatively slowly through some water that I could hear splashing underneath the utility. For the first minute or so we were on sealed roads but then it was back to gravel, unmade and rough surfaces.

I still had no sense of which direction we were heading. We could have been going north, south, east or west or any variation. I later discovered that we continued along The Grand Ridge Road.

Then more speeding, skidding, sliding, winding, braking and accelerating. Where on earth were we? And where on earth was he taking us?

It seemed like we drove for a long time.

>>><<<

It had been a normal morning for me, up until the intrusion. If after only nine days of teaching you can call anything normal. It was St Valentine's Day. Although I had a girlfriend at the time, the significance of the day wasn't on my mind. I had left my house in Mirboo North at 7.55am and driven the twenty minutes to school, enjoying the captivating countryside of rolling hills and well laid out farms. I arrived at school at about 8.15am. Some of the children were already there, having ridden their bikes. They were playing in the yard. I quickly prepared the morning lessons, writing up maths and handwriting exercises on the blackboard. It only being my second full week of teaching, I was still learning the ropes. I had been extremely nervous for the first few days of school, but had been greatly encouraged by the children's positive responses to both me and the lessons. I had a strong sense that this teaching business was my calling and that I was going to thoroughly enjoy the year with these delightful children.

I opened the doors to let the children in at 8.45am, although school didn't start until 9.15am. The children placed their bags on their respective hooks and put their books in their desks. One of the girls very kindly wished me a happy St Valentine's Day. Some wanted to chat with me about their weekend and various other matters of interest. I was happy to talk with them, however since I had more preparation to complete, I dismissed them after I had given each one some of my time. Some went back outside and a few stayed inside to read or do some other quiet activity.

When 9.15am came around, we started with the Patriotic Ceremony, outside in front of the flag. This involved singing the National Anthem and reciting the Oath of Allegiance. It promised to be a typical warm summer's day. There was some cloud cover, with virtually no breeze. After a brief walk around the yard, where the children and I discussed a variety of topics including eucalypts and habitats, we went back inside for more formal lessons at 9.30am. One of the children had picked some flowering gum, which they carefully arranged in a vase and placed on my table.

The children's cooperation, hard work and high level of interest in everything that we did made my role very straight-forward.

We started our classroom time with 'Morning Talk', where everybody took a turn at sharing something about their weekend. Then the older ones completed some handwriting exercises, followed by a current affairs activity with the daily newspaper. The younger children did some counting and number pattern work, with me directing them. I then set them to do some written number work by themselves in their work books, while I worked with the older children.

At 10.30am the children went outside for a fifteen-minute break. It was a usual primary school morning recess routine.

I said to the children, 'When you've completed your work, you can go outside.'

I had already checked some of the children's work, so I dismissed those particular children.

The remaining few were soon finished also.

'Mr. Hunter! I'm done,' Kay said.

I replied, 'Let me check… Yes, that's great Kay.'

'Maggie, well done! Lovely writing, you may go.'

'Ron, could you finish off that sentence, then you can get your morning recess.'

Having completed their tasks, off they all went. Some had gone to the toilet; others were chewing on their fruit or biscuit. One or two were preparing to play their favoured game of the month. The rest of them were still gathering their 'play lunch' and heading outside for some fresh air.

It was at that moment they came running back into the classroom, sounding the alarm to me regarding this intruding gunslinger. I still can't believe how such an ordinary morning turned into something from a horror film.

>>><<<

My knees and back hurt. I tried to change positions and sit partially on my thigh and bottom. I partly leant against the door but there were protrusions and knobs that pushed into my back. My throat felt dry and the acrid taste in my mouth was foul. The dust from the road seemed to be everywhere, up my nose, on my lips, in my mouth, all over my clothes, against my skin and all over the floor.

I could hear the children. They were distressed. I heard the sound of vomiting. They banged their hands against the wall between the two cabins as they called out, 'Stop!' 'Water!'

The gunman ignored them.

Oh Man! Don't you have a heart?

I asked, 'Have we got far to go? The kids are struggling in the back.'

'Not far to go,' he replied. 'I can't stop.'

I answered, 'But they're vomiting. They need a drink.'

'They've got milk to drink,' was the gunman's answer.

Oh yeah. Great! Idiot! The warm milk has probably made them sick.

The dust was shocking, getting in through every crack and space and filling the front cabin. It must have been even worse for the children in the back. Along with the smell and mess of their vomit, they would have also been covered in the dust. Breathing it in. Having it up their noses, in their mouths and down their throats. Being country kids, having driven on rough gravel roads they would have been used to the phenomena of dust in the car, but this was something else. The gunman had the window on my side of the utility partly down and I sensed that his had been down for most of the time. So, we did have some fresh air. There were no such options of opening any windows in the back.

I could hear other vehicles that we passed, from time to time. I could sense the intersections, where we had to slow to a crawl, then turn and proceed on. At a later stage the road seemed to get windier and our speed seemed to decrease, although we still travelled too quickly.

Through much of this time the gunman wanted to chat. I wasn't in the best frame of mind for this, but it did give me some sense of security that he wasn't about to do something to end my life. Not yet anyway. And it made him seem more human.

He told me that he had read about the Faraday kidnapping in the newspaper back in 1972 and that it had given him the idea for what he was now doing.

Great! Kidnapping! Doesn't sound very nice. Quite dramatic even.

I had some vague recollections of that kidnapping. There had been a lot of press. I'd been in form five in 1972 studying American history, economics and more.

This reference to 'kidnapping' and the use of the word took my thinking to a new level.

That's what is happening to me. Now!

I was being kidnapped along with my children. Even though the word 'kidnapping' had an impact, I still couldn't properly comprehend it.

All I knew was that I was tied up, blindfolded, painfully kneeling on the floor of a utility, that I was being driven by a madman, that the children and I had been forcibly taken against our wills, away from our little school, that my students, who I was guardian and protector of, were also tied up in the back, hurting, crying and vomiting, that we were being taken a long way from home and that I had no idea at all where on earth we were.

In particular, I thought about the parents, having their children stolen away. What would they think? How were they going to cope with this?

For a while we seemed to travel on a straighter road. The children were quiet.

'Where are you taking us?' I asked.

'I've got something not far away all set up for you,' he answered.

He explained that he had blankets and supplies, food and water that he had borrowed from a local establishment.

I wondered if he was indirectly suggesting that he'd stolen the supplies.

'What about this utility? Where does that come from?' I asked.

'Don't ask questions. There's some things you best not know.'

He talked about his dislike for Mr. Lindsay Thompson and the Education Department. For some reason, he had a set against both. It didn't make sense to me. I didn't know Mr. Thompson. All I knew was that he was the Acting Premier at the time and the Education Minister. As for the Education Department, they had generously paid me for three years during my teacher training and were now paying me even more generously to do a job that I loved. I didn't have any complaints.

He wanted to know how often the parents of the children came to the school to visit during the day. He was obviously wondering how effective his getaway had been and how long it would be before the police would be in chase. I too wondered how long it would take before the alarm would go off. I hoped that it would be sooner than later. Not being a very quick thinker, I explained that they didn't visit very much at all. I possibly should have told him they came consistently throughout the day, to get him worried. But I guess that wouldn't have done us any good either. It may have only exacerbated our precarious situation, which was about to become even worse.

From time to time I heard vehicles pass. I could tell that some were large trucks of a sort. Sometimes the gunman would slow right down to pass and at other times he would stop and pull over to allow them to pass. He would then get going again and increase to speeds that seemed much too fast for the rough road we were on.

We continued to drive rapidly around bends. By the revving of the engine and the changes in the forward and back movement of my weight, I could tell that we were going up and down some very steep inclines. Going up the hills my weight was pressed into the seat, but the downhill trajectory meant that at times I was pushed back towards the dash.

I could hear the gunman's movements. Clutch in and out. Gear lever, up and down. Shuffling in his seat. Different foot movements. Comments to himself about passing vehicles. I could then sense he was looking for something. Apparently, he was looking for his map. He couldn't find it. He rifled through his bag, leant over and squeezed past me to open the glove box. Eventually he stopped the vehicle to look for it properly.

The children called out, 'Ted, how much further to go? We need a drink of water.'

He yelled back that we didn't have too far to go and that he had some water at our destination.

The poor kids. All squashed in the back, thirsty. Although there were these few complaints and requests, they still seemed to be travelling without being totally distraught. Bless them!

He eventually found his map, possibly at the back of or under his seat. We then moved off again, a little slower than before, seemingly with him trying to read it as we went along. I could hear the crumpling, folding and unfolding of paper. He talked to himself out loud confirming to me that he was indeed reading his map and it appeared that he was unsure of the route.

He continued to stop from time to time to let other vehicles pass. The road was evidently very narrow and I could tell that it was not easy for some of the vehicles to get around.

I hoped that a driver in one of these vehicles would see our situation for what it was and raise the alarm.

>>><<<

I'd been rescued from near death previously, as a one-year-old child. I must have been some sort of an afterthought for my parents or perhaps, more likely, a big surprise, since my birth came six and a half years after Chris. All of my brothers loved their new little baby brother, however, when my eldest brother, Frank, found out that I was another boy, he wasn't too sure about my value. He was bitterly disappointed as he'd been hoping for a baby sister.

One day Ian and Chris, eight and seven years of age respectively, took me for a walk in my pusher. They walked me to the irrigation channel at the front of our house, where they became busily occupied with something of great interest. They had wheeled me into a prominent position on top of the channel bank and parked me there, leaving me for a time. Then to their dismay they heard behind them the distinct rattle, rustle and plunge of the pusher rolling down the bank, through the long grass and plunging into the channel. Down and under, went the pusher and I. Thankfully they were able to jump in and drag the pusher and me out. The story goes that when they guiltily told mum of the mishap, she was unruffled and took it all in her stride.

I was hoping that we could be saved in a similar fashion right now by someone noticing our plight.

>>><<<

On one occasion the gunman stopped to let another vehicle pass, except the approaching vehicle wouldn't go. He uttered something to the effect of, 'Come on mate, you'll fit.' But then he succumbed and had to reverse back a considerable distance into some larger space to let the vehicle through. In reversing he ended up backing into an embankment, which brought us to a sudden halt. Still facing backwards, I was thrust forward into the seat and then back again. Although I was unhurt it was still quite a jolt. The gunman swore. The children would have been thrust back and forth also. As the vehicle passed, I discerned that it must have been a large truck since the noise of the engine was significant. As the truck passed the gunman called out, 'She's right mate.'

I continued to wonder what these passing vehicles could see of the children in the back. I wondered too if the children weren't subtly trying to attract attention. I was unsure as to what the gunman could see of the children, but since they were under threat that if they didn't keep their heads down, 'bullets would be flying', I mused that they possibly wouldn't be doing too much.

In another instance around this time the gunman braked hard and skidded to a halt. He then hurriedly reversed for a short distance, braked again to a stop, turned sharp left and was on his way again at break-neck speed around corners and up and down hills. I continued to attempt to brace myself against the tossing and turning of the vehicle. The trouble was I never knew which way he was going to steer the vehicle next.

On we went. My position on the floor was increasingly uncomfortable. Everything hurt. Knees, back, shoulders, wrists and arms. My knees on the floor particularly hurt. I tried to change positions again and again by putting my weight on a different butt cheek. I was thirsty and the taste in my mouth and throat was awful. It wouldn't have been any better for the children.

I reasoned that the time was about 1.30pm. We had been away from the school for well over two hours. It seemed like we were a long way from Wooreen. We could have been anywhere. How would anyone ever find us at this place that he was taking us to? I hoped that someone had come to the school by now, that they had seen the clock stopped, the children's bags gone;

the phone tampered with, my personal things still there, and worked out that something was very wrong. I thought there was a reasonable chance of this happening.

I hoped that no one would be silly enough to get sucked into believing that damn note and just leave without checking out the school room. I felt that seeing the clock stopped at 11.10am and the sight of my wrist watch on my table would send alarm bells ringing. I thought that the watch in particular, left behind, would indicate that I hadn't departed the school voluntarily. Any teacher would ensure they had their watch with them when they left for an excursion. For comfort's sake, I had placed my watch on my work desk. It had become a usual practice that when I was settled in one place, I would take my watch off my wrist, as it was quite heavy and made my wrist ache. I hoped too that my wallet and keys sitting right by my watch would also get people thinking.

So, please, someone take notice of those signs and ring the police! We've been taken!

These scenarios, leading to our possible rescue, continued to cycle through my mind. But I never would have imagined what actually happened next.

Still travelling very fast, I could once again hear an oncoming vehicle. A loud one. Probably a large truck. Since we were going so fast, it was upon us quickly. Then, all in a moment, the gunman cursing... a sudden veering... brakes being applied... a hammering BANG! CRASH! Metal striking metal. I was thrust into the side and then the front of the vehicle. The back of my head thumped the front of the van, my shoulder against the door. There were screams from the children in the back... I heard the children being thrown against the sides and front of the rear cabin. Then we were moving backwards, more curses from the gunman, more sounds of metal grinding against metal. It seemed like we were being pushed by something in front of us. I could sense the gunman trying to brake and steer but there was this continued push backwards… further backwards… then more scraping and grinding at front and back and side and then we stopped, and there was silence.

PART TWO

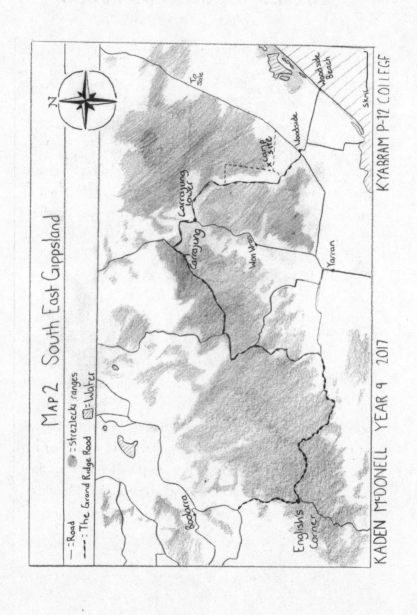

MAP 2 South East Gippsland

Key:
— = Road
● = Strezlecki ranges
---- = The Grand Ridge Road
▨ = Water

N

To Sale

Woodside Beach

Woodside

Camp Site

Carrajung Lower

Carrajung

Won Wron

Yarran

Boolarra

English's Corner

ENGLISH'S CORNER: 1.35PM

I'd only previously experienced one slight accident in my twenty years.

I was about fourteen when I had the accident. My parents, two of my adult brothers and I were living in town and so there were four vehicles constantly in the garage and driveway, on the front lawn and on the street at the front of our house. When the other two older brothers visited there were even more vehicles about. I was always very happy to volunteer to shuffle cars around and to unblock a car that had other cars behind it. I thought I was an expert driver. It was one of the benefits of being a farm kid. The opportunities to practice were endless with a variety of machines that needed operating and there was space available to experiment. Dad was very eager for all us boys to learn as early as possible. I'd certainly been given more than my share of learning experiences. I think Dad worked on the theory of 'practice makes perfect'. Some of my earliest memories are of Dad sitting me on the tractor to steer around a paddock. He would set the tractor going in a low gear, put me in the driver's seat, then jump down to the ground, climb on to the trailer behind and feed out the hay for the cows. I might have been as young as four or five at the time.

On the day of my first accident, I needed to reverse Dad's utility out of the driveway and onto the street to allow Mum to get the family car out. I approached the task with my usual confidence. With great dexterity, I turned my body to look behind.

As I was finishing reversing out of the driveway, I turned the utility sharply to align it with the parking space in the street, all the while looking behind me to make sure that I was heading correctly into the parking space. Crunch! There was a loud sound of the car hitting against a firm object. To my astonishment the front mud guard of the utility had caught hard against a post on the side fence, causing significant damage to the utility, but thankfully minimal damage to the fence.

Upon telling Dad the bad news, he was unbelievably forgiving. Hardly raising a frown, he uttered such words as, 'Son, we learn by our mistakes.'

>>><<<

Here in my blindfold, I was in a totally different kind of accident. The engine was off. I could hear hissing – steam and water escaping from the radiator, I assumed. We'd hit a large truck, I guessed.

My head and shoulder hurt. Had I lost a moment? Blacked out? I wasn't aware of losing time.

The gunman was cursing and muttering about, 'Bloody logging trucks.'

I could hear the children moving in the back. There was crying and sobbing. I wondered how badly they were hurt.

I could hear the gunman trying to get out of the vehicle: the driver's door wouldn't open. More cursing, yanking, pushing, banging. Eventually, I heard him awkwardly trying to climb out through his side window with lots of grunting and groaning. I heard him land on the ground and begin to move quickly away.

Exclamations and shouts followed. They were men's voices, from some distance away. I was able to decipher parts of the conversation.

'Sorry mate,' I heard the gunman call out.

Pause.

Followed by, 'Get your hands in the air.'

An exclamation from another voice, 'What's this…?'

'Come back here or I'll shoot!'

There were some quieter voices but I couldn't make out the words. It seemed that there were two men that the gunman was dealing with from the truck.

Soon after the gunman yelled, 'Get down! On the road! Face down! Flat! Both of you! Hands straight out, above your head!'

'Don't try anything fucking smart or I'll blow your heads off.'

Some of the children were crying.

Oh man! Those poor kids!

'Are you guys alright?' I called? 'Can you hear me? Is anyone seriously hurt?'

'We're alright, Mr. Hunter. It's just Ron. He hit his head. We all got thrown around.' I thought it was Maggie talking to me.

'Is Ron okay?' I asked.

'He'll be okay,' someone else answered back.

I could hear them consoling each other. Questions being asked of each other. Comforting. Sobbing.

They were saying, 'Are you okay?'

'It's only a small graze.'

'You'll be alright.'

'It'll be okay.'

I reckoned it would have been Maggie, Lucy, Jill and Leanne making sure that all the younger ones were safe and reassured.

I could hear Lucy announcing something to the effect that we were hanging over the edge of a big drop and telling the rest of the children that they all needed to stay as still as possible or we might go over the edge. If that were true, it would be a real worry, I thought. However, it felt to me like the utility was quite stable. There was no further movement of the vehicle, so I assumed that it was simply a childish concern.

Outside, I couldn't hear any activity. I pictured two captive men, lying on the road, face down in the gravel with the gunman standing over them gaining his thoughts, assessing his options.

We'd obviously had an accident. How bad it was I wasn't entirely sure. It didn't seem like anyone was too seriously hurt. I was alive. The children seemed to be okay despite the crying. The gunman didn't seem to be hurt, even though his door was apparently jammed or smashed shut.

The gunman would have been peeved with this accident interfering with his getaway to his destination. He would also have been concerned about the problem of what to do with two extra men and the possibility of us all overpowering him. Mind you, still being blindfolded, tied up and sitting on the floor of this now decrepit vehicle, I wasn't too much of a threat. But the blokes from the truck; well, that was another matter. I assumed they were totally unrestrained at present.

The children continued to care for each other in the back. The crying seemed to be abating. The supportive Rural School family atmosphere was continuing. The care the older ones were giving the younger children was comforting.

Beautiful children. Amazingly, they were remaining incredibly calm. They seemed to be coping with this awful set of events, which was only getting worse by the minute, with unbelievable composure.

I could hear the gunman's voice: it was closer now. It seemed like he was moving the guys closer to where we were, near his utility. Orders and threats were made to the men again. 'Lie there! Don't you blokes try anything or I'll blow your brains out.'

He seemed to walk to the rear of our vehicle. He spoke to the children, asking them if they were okay. I guessed he was keeping an eye on the truck drivers at the same time. He was planning to get the children out of the vehicle.

Getting the kids out of the back of the utility was not going to happen easily. I didn't know this at the time, but we were actually in a perilous position. Lucy's concern about being over the edge of a big drop was absolutely right. The gunman couldn't access the rear of the vehicle because it was partly suspended over a precipice. Below the vehicle was a drop of sixty to eighty metres. The vehicle was sitting at a precarious angle with the back-left wheel hanging out over the edge of this drop. The undercarriage of the vehicle was being supported by the verge of the road. My door was also inaccessible as there was a massive drop beneath it. That the vehicle was still on the road was a miracle. A white, four or five-inch square, solid wooden post, on the side of the road was helping prop up the vehicle near my door. This post was stopping us from going over the edge; not that I could see any of this at that moment.

Upon reflection, we were so fortunate! It seemed too miraculous for us to have wound up in that precise position, held only by the white post.

The gunman couldn't get the children out the back of the vehicle through the hatches because of the massive drop. He couldn't get them out through the front cabin since the window into the back was fixed. He decided that the best way to reach the children was through the right-hand window of their cabin. This window was little more than thirty centimetres in height and eighty centimetres long. There were two of these windows, one beside the other. Like the window between the front and back cabins they were fixed windows, with no winding or sliding option. Glass would need to be broken to get anyone through.

I could sense that the gunman was agitated and in a hurry.

He spoke tersely to the children, telling them that to get out of the vehicle they would have to climb out through the window. Then he was ordering them to move back, away from the window, while he smashed it in.

How are they going to move back out of the way? For goodness sake! They're already in a confined space.

Having told the children to move back as far as possible, the gunman smashed the window inwards. I could hear broken glass spill everywhere. I could well imagine the danger that the gunman had just put the children in again, by smashing the glass all over them.

Hell! What next?

The chances of one of the children being seriously cut was high.

I found out later that he had used the butt of his gun to smash the window. Somehow no one had received any major injuries.

From my jail I continued to listen.

The children were guided and supported out of the vehicle, all the while dodging the broken glass. The string of nine now seemed to be only partly secured together by the chain and padlocks. It appeared that a number of them had somehow managed to get their hands out of the chain.

I heard the gunman say to Kay, 'How did you get your hand out of the chain?'

'It just fell off,' she said.

It sounded like a good answer to me.

Good on you kids!

The gunman was guiding them through the window. I found it hard to understand how they could physically fit through the small window that I had glimpsed back at the school. There must have been significant contorting of bodies for them to get through such a small opening.

I could hear the gunman telling the children to put their feet in certain positions as they wormed their way out. Some were still joined by the chain. I could hear the scraping of metal as it dragged against the utility. One by one I heard them landing on the ground. The older ones were helping the younger.

The children were then made to lie face down on the road not far from the men.

'Lie down there! On your fronts. In a row, just like those blokes,' the gunman ordered.

I assumed they did exactly what he said. They were well practiced in lining up, standing in rows. The older children would always ensure that the younger were in line correctly. I guessed they would be able to lie down in line also.

I wondered what the gunman might do with me. It was always on my mind that he might rid himself of the teacher.

Perhaps he might leave me right here.

But no, not yet, my time wasn't up. He came back to the driver's window and spoke to me.

'Are you alright Teach?'

Oh yeah! Sure! I'm great! A knock to the head. Cramps in my legs. A sore shoulder. You've had me tied up here for two and a half hours. What do you think?

But once again, rather submissively I said, 'I'm fine.'

'Let's get you out of there,' he said. 'We've got a problem, though. Your door is over a bloody great chasm and my door is stuffed!' He paused for a moment. 'I'll have to untie you.'

He asked me to climb up onto the seat. With considerable effort I managed to unravel my cramped limbs, turn and slide up onto the seat. He leant in through the window towards me saying that he would first remove my blindfold, which he did. With a quick tug, he pulled the sticking plaster from my eyes.

Ouch! More plucked hair!

But oh! I could see! Light! It seemed incredibly bright.

My eyes took some seconds to make the adjustment. The first thing I noticed was the gunman leaning in through the window reaching out towards me with a pocket knife in hand. Thankfully there was no malice in his intent.

I saw his intense dark eyes and unshaven face. He looked rushed, anxious and totally absorbed in the moment.

His only intention seemed to be to free me from the vehicle.

All in a split-second I saw my immediate surrounds. I saw his red bag right next to me. The shabby untidy cabin. The mangled bonnet of the utility pushed up in the air in front of our windscreen. The Gippsland bush, green and vibrant through the windows. A steep embankment on the other side of the road. Nothing except the tops of trees outside my window. A large logging truck right next to us.

He worked at ridding me of my ropes. He first cut the ropes from around my waist, but my hands remained secure behind my back. The ropes were still taut and had been wound around a number of times and so untying me was a tricky task. He still must have been concerned about the two men not too far away from him, who were still lying face down on the road. I assume this is why he worked in such a rush. The ropes needed to be unravelled. I'm not too sure what he did, but as he unravelled the length of rope it ran hard and fast against the skin of my wrists, rubbing roughly, abrasively. Burning.

Although it didn't cause excessive pain at the time, the burning effect was very real. The burn marks are still with me today, a lifelong memento of those traumatic events, just like the emotional scars that still mark the children and me today.

The gunman continued working at freeing me from the vehicle.

Strange as it may seem, the gunman was now my rescuer. The irony of this didn't totally escape me but I certainly didn't have time to dwell on it!

Should I have been thankful for his efforts?

The gunman explained that I needed to climb out his window. Having been able to move from the floor to the seat, I now continued to move myself from my seat towards the window. I'd been cramped on the floor of the utility for about two and a half hours. It felt strange to be able to straighten my legs, arms, hands and my whole body. Everything felt stiff and my initial movements were slow and rather awkward.

I wormed my way up onto the window, closely watched by my kidnapper come rescuer.

I sat for the briefest of moments on the window frame of the door getting my bearings, enjoying a small sense of freedom. My legs were free. My hands and arms were free. It was a good feeling. The gunman stood well back with gun in hand, waiting for me to jump down.

I saw the two guys lying face down on the road with the children next to them also lying face down, some of them still joined by the chain. The four older girls, Maggie, Lucy, Jill and Leanne were there. The two grades three and four girls too, Bernie and Kay. And the three boys, Ron, Russell and Dale. All children accounted for. Good!

I was also able to gain a further appreciation of where we were.

Thick bushland. Mountains. Huge logging truck. Very narrow gravel road.

Then swivelling on my bottom, I pulled my legs through from inside the car to the outside and jumped onto the ground. My legs and feet still worked.

Like the gunman had instructed the two men before me and just as he had ordered me a few hours before, he told me to lie face down with my arms outstretched above my head.

The gunman barked, 'Lie there! All three of you. Don't try anything fucking smart or I'll shoot you!'

He said this as he moved over towards the children.

My face was almost in the dirt. I rested my head partly on my outstretched arm and tried not to breathe in the dust from the road.

Lifting my head slightly, I was now able to see more clearly where we were, what we had hit and the state of our vehicle.

The truck was a timber jinker, a logging truck with three or four massive great logs on the back. The logs were about a metre thick at one end and just under a metre thick at the other. They must have been about twelve to fifteen metres long. The whole truck with such a load made it an extremely heavy weight; not something that could be stopped in a hurry. No wonder it had pushed us so far backwards. The rear axle with four massive wheels was just to my left. The back-right tyre was flat and the wheel rim badly damaged from the impact with the utility.

I could see that we had collided on a very sharp bend, on an extremely narrow gravel road in what appeared to be the most isolated, remote place imaginable, with thick, lush and green bushland that was all around us. Behind me was a very steep incline, heavily wooded with numerous towering, perfectly straight eucalypts. The road had been dug into the side of the mountain by some aggressive engineering process. In front of me, past the wreck of the utility, there was thick vegetation going down, down, down! There was a massive drop! From my position on the ground, all I could see were the tops of tree ferns and the sides of tree trunks and the high foliage of trees disappearing down a very steep embankment.

There was a thick layer of leaf litter on the side of the road in front of me. Green grass with a range of small flowering plants and a smattering of bracken fern also lined the edge of the road. The vibrant tree ferns adorned the beginning of the steep downward slope. The constant sound of birds tweeting and what sounded to me like bell birds filled the air. The breeze meant there was a continuous rustling sound in the gum trees. I could hear the sound of frogs croaking. There was also the piercing loud noise of cicadas.

The Dodge utility was in a sorry state – the front right all smashed in. The bonnet was pushed up in front of the windscreen, almost totally obscuring any view from the front seats. It was an absolute mess. It certainly wasn't going any further along that road today.

The truck and utility had formed a complete road block. The nose of the truck was very close to the embankment on the left-hand side of the road and the crumpled utility was less than a metre from the back of the truck on the right-hand side. We were on a hair pin bend in the road.

The gunman's vehicle was sitting at a precarious angle on the edge of the precipice. The undercarriage of the vehicle continued to be supported by the edge of this steep drop, which appeared to go down more than sixty metres. A veritable cliff! How close had we been to going over that edge? I was still unaware of the post jammed up just behind my door. Had that enormous truck pushed us another few centimetres towards the edge we may well have all been pounded in a plummeting descent.

How ironic it would have been to have survived the kidnapping but then died in a collision. I was aware of many examples of such occurrences in life. People who had survived a war and then gone home to die in an accident or from some other random event.

Mum and Dad would have prayed for me that morning. They prayed for me every day. Were we saved by the prayers of my parents and others that day?

'G'day,' I whispered to the guys next to me.

With arms still outstretched and with heads partly raised, resting on our upper arms, pleasantries between us three captives were exchanged. In soft voices, some introductions and brief comments and queries about what was taking place were made. It was both strange and comforting to be able to talk to some other regular people.

The two men were Robin Smith, the driver of the timber jinker, and David Smith, his passenger and younger brother.

'Where are you from?' they asked.

'Who is he?'

'How did he capture you?'

'What's he want?'

The two guys' baffled, quick-fire questions in hushed voices brought me into a more acute awareness that this outlandish event was truly taking place. They were both totally confounded by the situation. Unsurprisingly, they had never heard of Wooreen. As to the gunman's identity, at this point I still only knew the name 'Ted'. I explained to the two guys that the gunman had told the children to call him 'Ted'. I tried to answer their questions with reasonable answers but everything I said seemed to only add to the bizarre nature of what was happening. In whispers I tried to explain how he had burst into our school, having rounded the kids up from outside and then tied us up and bundled us into his utility.

I didn't think I had done a very good job of answering their mystified questions.

Robin explained to me that his truck was now not drivable. Ted had ripped the wires out from under the dash because he was concerned about the two-way radio that Robin had.

They seemed like typical, strong, hardworking Aussie guys. They were both clean shaven with fair hair and of slightly below average height and of average build. I guessed that they were in their late twenties, both older than me. They were wearing shorts, with work boots. I had a sense that they were both mature, sensible men who would do anything to help out a mate. Having them there with me gave me the first sense that things would turn out okay. They were a great comfort.

I wondered if they could smell me. The stink of vomit lingered in my nostrils however the horrible taste in my mouth and my burning throat had almost disappeared. They might not have smelt it, but they certainly noticed, since the mess was still evident down the front of my shirt and possibly my beard.

'You've been sick,' commented David, lying next to me.

'Yeah. Spewed my guts out!' I replied.

We lay there face down with arms still outstretched, heads resting on our arms, trying not to take in the dust from the road, and waited. For what, we didn't know.

Communication with the children at this point was virtually impossible. I looked in their direction. Ted was unlocking the chain from Russell's wrist. They were a few metres to my right. Having released Russell's wrist, Ted began sorting through his pile of keys trying to find the appropriate key for the next lock. His gun was sitting in his back-right pocket.

Bernie exchanged a brief passing smile with me.

The children looked dirty and dishevelled. They had just gone through the ride of their lives. They looked tired. Some of their heads were down. They looked bewildered and troubled.

Ron was holding his head back and was squeezing his nose with his fingers, dealing with a blood nose. There appeared to be blood around his shirt.

They were no longer being forced to lie down. Most were standing near Ted, and the couple that remained chained were waiting to be untied. After the last child was unlocked they were instructed to move over to the side of the road and sit at the foot of the embankment, further away, behind us and to our right. There they were allowed to sit in relative freedom away from us men.

Ted was putting the keys in one front pocket and the locks in the other. His gun continued to rest in his back pocket.

What was he going to do now?

Surely, he will give up and go home, won't he? Give up this game as a bad joke.

He must have been wondering what he was going to do too, now that he had no vehicle to transport us in.

How is he going to be able to complete his stupid stunt?

I was feeling significantly more confident with two blokes beside me. I didn't think he would shoot three of us. Surely not!

Three men. Nine children. The odds seemed to be growing in my favour.

However, the possibility of my life ending was still on my mind. I had a strong faith in what Jesus had done for me on the cross and I fully believed that He had beaten death by His coming back to life. I celebrated it every Easter. If Ted shot me at this moment I felt confident that my eternal state was safe, in God's hands.

Even so, I still didn't want to die. I had my whole life ahead of me. And I certainly didn't want to be shot in front of the children. I didn't want anyone shot! The gun, however, continued to threaten us all.

Will he take the children with the next vehicle that comes along and leave us men behind? Perhaps he might dispose of us men over the edge. Will he escape in the next vehicle and leave us all here?

Still considering these possibilities, I watched as he continued to finish sorting out his keys and locks along with the chain. He rushed. He must have been concerned about who might come or what we three blokes might do.

Once completed, Ted moved over to the three of us lying flat on our fronts in the middle of the road, with the chain in his hands. The end of the chain dragged behind him, clattering on the rough gravel road. His gun had returned to his front-right pocket.

'This chain is now for you. I'm not taking any risks with you blokes.'

I was going to be tied up by the chain again. I resigned myself to the inevitability of the process. It was much better than being blindfolded, gagged and tied up with hands and arms behind my back, forced to kneel on the floor of a utility, facing backwards while he drove like crazy around unmade windy roads. I was still feeling relatively free and having these other two blokes with me, my spirits had been bolstered considerably.

Ted proceeded to chain each of us up.

The reality of what was happening continued to lightly wash over me. It was as if I was in Fantasyland.

Is this a dream? This can't really be happening to me, can it?

I'd lived a pretty normal life. Home, farm, parents, brothers, school, college, church, cricket, footy, mates, the occasional girlfriend, a few problems, lots of good times, some hard work, a few mistakes, a bit of trouble… but this! This was unreal! It was the start of my teaching career and I was being forced to lie on a gravel road face down with two blokes I'd never met. I'd almost been killed in an accident; my life had been threatened. It was possible that I could be shot and killed at any moment, my nine students were captives also…

What the heck?

However, the reality was that I was about to be chained again. But firstly, Robin.

Ted warned, 'Lie still now, boys. Hands and arms straight out in front. Don't try anything smart. I'm happy to shoot. There will be claret running down the gutter if you make any false moves.'

After Ted had attached the chain and padlock to Robin's left wrist Ted looked at him and said, 'Hey Singlet! I know you, don't I? Where do I know you from?'

Robin was wearing a grubby blue singlet, the sort that Australian truck drivers wear. Commonly known as a 'Bluey', the singlet was becoming distinctly grubbier lying on the gravel road. He was not a big man. He was noticeably smaller and lighter in weight than Ted, certainly too light to overpower Ted by himself.

Robin responded with, 'No! Sorry! I don't know you.'

Ted argued the point, challenging Robin, suggesting that they had been in the clink together or that there had been some other encounter. Ted pursued the matter saying that he didn't trust Robin, accusing him of having shifty eyes and an untrustworthy face. Finally, Ted warned him not to try to be a smart ass. Robin hardly responded, choosing to remain silent. He kept his head down and looked at the gravel road in front of his face.

Ted added, 'I'll be watching you like a hawk. Try anything and I'll shoot you.'

It was a curious altercation and accusation. Perhaps it was the springboard to prompt Robin to start thinking about how he might undo Ted.

David was padlocked up next, followed by me. We were each secured to the chain by our left wrist only, just as the children had been. The chain was first looped around our wrist and then the padlock was used to join up two links, ensuring that this silver dog chain was tight around the narrowest part of our arms. Our attachments to the chain were about a metre from the next person's.

Ted padlocked the end of the chain to the back of the truck, nearest to Robin.

Having secured the three of us, Ted moved back over to his utility and began retrieving his bag and various other belongings.

Looking behind me and to my right I checked on the children. A quick count indicated that all nine were there. They were together in one group on the other side of the road, about fifteen metres or so from us men. Some sitting. Some standing.

After a few more minutes, we heard the sound of another vehicle approaching from the same direction that we had come from. Another sizeable truck was nearing: the roar of the engine and the changing of gears were obvious tell-tale signs.

Ted was on full alert.

Louder and louder the noise became. Presumably another logging truck. Robin and David indicated that they knew who and what it was likely to be.

Confirming that his gun was well hidden down the back of his trousers, in the centre of his back, Ted left us at the tail end of the logging truck, walked along the left side of the trailer and approached the oncoming truck some forty metres or more from our position.

I wasn't able to see the truck, but I guessed that it would have stopped in the middle of the road, ten or so metres in front of Robin's truck.

From our distance, we could partly make out the conversation between Ted and what we assumed would have been a man, as the driver of the truck.

Again, there was the affable preliminary chatter.

'G'day! Can you give us a hand? There's been an accident,' called Ted.

We listened intently.

It seemed that no sooner than whoever was in the truck was getting out, that Ted pointed the gun at them.

'Get your hands in the air!'

We heard a stifled, surprised response. Very shortly, we saw two men approaching with hands in the air. Ted was behind them, gun in hand, pointing at their backs. Another two men were on board! For Ted, it seemed to me that this was getting out of hand.

A string of threats followed for all of the men:

'Just do what I fucking say and no one will get hurt.'

'We don't want to scare the kids, do we?'

'I'm very happy to shoot any of you if need be. Just try me!'

'Lie down there. Face down. Arms straight out above your heads.'

'No funny business.'

Wisely, these two new guys did as requested, with puzzled and surprised looks. They lay face down on the road alongside us three, to my right.

Ted promptly secured them to our chain. The first guy's left wrist was fastened a metre down the chain from mine. The same routine: loop, padlock, click. The second guy was then chained in like manner. Now there were five men lying face down on the road with arms outstretched, all chained together. Surely now Ted would give up and flee. This was ridiculous! But no, he had come this far, he wasn't giving up so easily. He was evidently a desperate man, hell-bent on pursuing his absurd intentions.

Ted wandered over to the children, checking on them.

Once again, we began quiet, stilted conversations with the two new guys. Robin and David knew the driver of this second truck well. His name was Greg Peterson. In fact, the truck he was driving was owned by Robin. Greg was working for him. It was another timber jinker, only this one was without a load. Greg's passenger, Ian Webber, who was now lying next to me face down in the dirt, was only seventeen years old.

Greg was obviously puzzled and asked us a series of questions, all at once.

'Where are you from? What happened? Who is he? What's he want?'

It was a weird conversation for a range of reasons. Not only were we whispering, we were also very conscious of where Ted was and unsure of how much we would be allowed to talk. We were all lying flat on our bellies, face down on the gravel road, with the smell of earth up our nostrils. I was positioned in the middle of the five men, Greg on one end of the chain and Robin on the other end, who knew each other very well. The stifled and inter-mittent discussion continued depending on where Ted was. Most of the questions were directed at me from Greg. I answered as best I could while Robin and David chimed in with their perspectives.

The guys confirmed that we were in an extremely remote place.

The words 'kidnapped', 'captive' and 'ransom' were used and very briefly discussed.

A fuller realisation as to what was actually happening began to form in my mind as we conversed. In explaining and putting into words what was taking place, a new understanding emerged. Interacting with these men helped bring about a new perspective and a clearer sense of what was really happening. I knew from the start that I had been kidnapped by a bloke with a gun but much of its truth had been lost on me in the rush of events.

It may seem obvious to the reader what was going on but up to that point it was only the immediate confronting things that had dominated my thinking. My thoughts had centred on the fact that myself and the children, who I was supposed to be looking after and teaching, were being taken away from our school by a bloke with a gun. It was only now, as I began conversations with these other blokes who, like me, were now captive, that the reality and some of the ramifications of the situation began to become clear. I began to realise the enormity of the crime that was taking place, the effect that this was going to have on families and friends and the important role of the police.

I think that I'd been experiencing denial as some kind of coping mechanism up to this point just to come to terms with what had been happening, because it was all so far removed from my experience of reality. A kidnapping seemed like something that only ever happened to other people, distant from me.

Although I felt some comfort from the camaraderie of these men, I knew we were still in a very desperate situation. Our lives were in the balance.

The truck drivers knew the road and understood exactly where we were. We were very close to English's Corner, which was somewhere between Tarra Valley, Boolarra and some other places that I hadn't heard of. I had some knowledge of Boolarra, having seen it on a signpost or two in my travels over those first two weeks, and I'd seen it on a map, but not so the other places.

The guys wanted to know what time the parents were likely to become aware of our absence and how long it would be before an alert went out. It was the big question. I only had eight days of routine to go by. In those eight days I could only recall one time when a parent had visited the school during the day and that was to drop off a forgotten lunch. Would there be a forgotten lunch call today? It wasn't likely. The children hadn't mentioned anything along those lines. I tried to explain to the guys that I had only been teaching at the school for little more than a week. They showed their surprise. However, there was so much to be surprised about at this point that it was only given passing notice. I also explained to them the note on the door. They seemed to recognise the seriousness of our predicament.

Ted came back to us.

'Stop talking! Don't even think about any funny business. Just remember who's got the power here. Do anything fucking smart and you're dead.'

Lucy walked over to where we were and asked Ted if she could have her school bag as it had some books in it that she and some of the others wanted to read. He obliged. Reaching into the utility with a stick through the window he retrieved the bag and gave it to Lucy.

He walked along the road to where the two timber jinkers sat head to head. We could hear him opening and closing the doors of the trucks. I wondered what he was searching for.

He came back with an axe and a sleeping bag in his hands saying, 'These might be useful. It pays to be resourceful.'

They had come from Robin's truck and evidently belonged to him. Robin didn't comment. I guess there was little point in saying much. Certainly, no point in protesting.

He placed the axe and sleeping bag on the road with his red bag of goodies.

So, there we lay, five men against our wills lying face down in the middle of the dusty road, chained to each other with our arms above our heads. It was not a comfortable position.

Five men against one. Surely, Ted would give up this absurdity.

He stood close by. Talk was impossible.

How might we escape? There didn't seem to be any chance.

For goodness sake! Run away! There's five of us blokes and only one of you. Give up!

Where would he run to though? Where would he go? Greg had mentioned something about him being a 'con'. Ted had also suggested that he'd met Robin in prison. Was he an escaped prisoner?

As a young boy I distinctly remembered the story of some escapees from Pentridge Prison in Melbourne being on the run. The newspapers and radio reports indicated that they were in northern Victoria somewhere. The police had been in hot pursuit. They warned the general population of the danger of approaching these desperate men. The talk in our family was that perhaps they could end up in Kyabram and hide on our farm. As I recall, they were apprehended on a farm a few miles south of Kyabram, hiding in a farmer's hay stack. I had been intrigued by the saga.

I suspected that I was now at the mercy of a similarly desperate man.

We waited.

At one point Ted walked over to the smashed utility, put his back to it and began to rock it back and forth, attempting to push it over the edge. From our vantage point, it seemed that it should go over easily. He was able to get the utility to rock back and forwards substantially, but it wouldn't go over the edge.

I offered to help him push it over.

He declined.

Why did I do that? I immediately felt quite foolish for offering to help a kidnapper.

Upon reflection it was pretty silly of me to offer my assistance. Impetuous? Reckless? Wanting more excitement? Wanting to be helpful? Wanting to stretch the limits? I'm not really sure but it was a little typical of my character to dive in the deep end.

Obscured from us all was the white post, supporting the vehicle from its otherwise inevitable plunge. It was a strong post and well embedded in the ground. Not like the flimsy plastic ones of today.

Ted was probably thinking that in disposing of the utility down the precipice, he could hide the clues of our whereabouts from the police, knowing that they would certainly be on our trail at some stage. However, being unsuccessful in pushing the utility over the edge, he soon abandoned the idea.

As a second-best option Ted unscrewed the number plates from the utility and placed them in his bag.

I wondered how far away the police might be. I gauged that it was about 2.00 in the afternoon. It was possible that someone had come to the school and set off an alarm and begun the search. As much as I hoped that to be the case, I knew that it was more probable that no one would turn up to the school until 3.30pm, at the end of the school day. Then they would read the note and not worry too much, for a while. At best, I reasoned the police wouldn't be notified until 4.00pm. How were they going to know where we were? This accident site would be the first clue, I supposed.

The children were on the edge of the road unrestrained, in the shade of the thick foliage behind and to the right of where we men were lying about twenty metres away. Most of them were sitting on the edge of the road with their feet in the gutter at the foot of the cutting. A couple of them were now reading, presumably the books from Lucy's bag that Ted had retrieved for her. Russell was throwing stones at the bank in front of them. The family atmosphere continued to be present as they sat or stood close together in a tight group. Having been through so much in the last few hours and not having had anything substantial to eat or drink, they were doing surprisingly well. I knew that a number of them had been car sick and vomited, but I wasn't sure how many. What was going through their minds now? What were they feeling? The camaraderie that seemed to be constantly evident was most encouraging for me, being so cut off from them.

I was to find out later that they had found a number of leeches amongst the thick vegetation in the gutter. Some of the children had poked, prodded and squashed them like any kids would have done upon finding such interesting little creatures. There would have been the normal 'Oohs!' and 'Aahs!' and other exclamations of dislike at the blood sucking critters.

At about this time one of the girls, a quietly conscientious child, approached me in front of all the men.

She said, 'Mr. Hunter. I need to go to the toilet.'

She had left the group of children momentarily and walked over to where we men were lying on the ground.

Oh yes! Of course! Toilet. Why hadn't I been thinking of that for these poor kids? How had they all hung on for so long?

I was mindful of the fact that they had brought their lunches with them and that Ted had encouraged them to drink the cartons of milk that he had in the back of the utility.

So how had they all not needed to go to the toilet before this? Had the boys simply turned away from the group and quickly done their business perhaps?

How is Ted going to respond to this appeal?

Qualifying her call of needing the toilet, she said to me, 'I only need to have a wee.'

I was particularly impressed with her confidence and trust in me, that she would make this appeal in front of the men. She was also risking Ted's wrath, by leaving the place where she had been directed to be and walked over to us.

Such a simple but vitally normal request. Bless her! What a gutsy effort. This is a tricky one. How can I make this happen for her? How can I make this easy for her?

Raising myself slightly by bringing my hands back level with my shoulders, I said, 'Good on you! I'll ask Ted if he'll let you go around the corner.'

Ted was leaning against the embankment behind us and partly to my left, on the far side of the truck.

Turning around slightly and partly looking in his direction, I called, 'Excuse me, Ted. This girl needs to have a wee, can she please go around the corner?'

Come on mate! This trusting and vulnerable young girl needs to keep her dignity intact. Have a heart!

But no. This young child's life and self-esteem wasn't as important as this madman's ridiculous stunt.

Ted directed her to go behind the back wheels of the timber jinker, not much more than about five metres from where I was lying. This was to the right side of the truck, between the truck and the wrecked utility.

Mercifully, I was unable to see her squatting but I'm not sure about the other men or all the other children. There was no mention of toilet paper. The trickle of urine wound its way across the road through the dirt and stones in our general direction but slightly to our left.

Having relieved herself, she probably felt a relief in one sense, however her self-image and confidence must have taken an absolute beating. I imagine she was mortified to have to urinate, not only in close proximity to her friends, but nearby six strange, grown men.

I felt so helpless! The poor kid having to bare all in such circumstances. How demeaning! How cruel! It made me angry.

At the same time, I was proud of her sense of composure and calm, on the outside at least. She, along with the other older children, continued to be so unruffled and cool and so caring and supportive of the younger students.

As she was returning to the rest of the children she had to walk back past us.

I said, 'Well done! Are the rest of the kids okay? Do any of the others need to go to the toilet?'

'They're good. Kay has a small cut from the glass but she's okay. I'll check about them needing the toilet.'

Ted seemed to be fine with this interchange, which gave me confidence that I could talk to the children some more.

Pushing my luck and somewhat fearful of a back-lash from Ted, I called out to them. 'You kids okay? Anyone else need to go to the toilet?'

Heads moved in our direction. There were some smiles and acknowledgments from different ones. Again, some of the older children checking on the younger ones. They seemed to be alright and no one indicated that they needed to go to the toilet. I wondered if any of the other five girls may have needed to go to the toilet but were simply too embarrassed to do what their peer had just gone through. If that was the case, I didn't blame them one bit.

There we all waited for who knew what. The other men and I had been able to change our arm positions without Ted commenting. We had brought our hands and arms back level with our heads and shoulders, which was more comfortable. There we rested our heads.

I was hungry and thirsty, not having had anything to eat or drink since I had left home that morning before eight o'clock. I was very aware of my dirty and smelly state. My shabby beard had certainly caught some of the discharge when I'd thrown up, ensuring that the odour was never far from my senses. The dust and dirt that was also all over my clothes, my skin and through my hair and beard masked the intensity of the stench, however.

The children remained in their place on the side of the road. The three boys were now standing, picking up stones and sticks from near their feet and throwing them onto the embankment. One of the girls was pulling at the grass at the side of the road and chewing it. Ted didn't seem to be too worried about their movements.

It was a warm day. Not particularly hot. A very light breeze ensured the constant swirl in the trees. There was a cloud cover, which, along with the canopy of the massive eucalypts, ensured that we were fully protected from any direct effects of the sun. Beautiful vegetation dominated this remote place and birds continued to make their presence known through continuous song.

As time passed I became increasingly aware of our remoteness and isolation. No other vehicles. No sounds other than the normal bush noises. We were in the middle of nowhere, it seemed. Ted had certainly opted for the back route to wherever he was taking us.

He stayed behind us, moving between the embankment and the timber jinker, his gun neatly placed in his front right pocket. The end of the butt protruded, with the barrel bedded deeply in his pocket. He continued to wear his gloves. For much of this time he worked at whittling away a green stick with his pocket knife while leaning against the truck just behind us and to the left. I wasn't sure whether this was purely a passing-the-time, idle activity or whether he had something in mind. Was he demonstrating something to us, his captives? Wanting to give us a message? The ground all around the back left of the truck where he was standing was covered in small green shavings from where he had been whittling away.

Whenever Ted moved away a little, the other blokes and I discussed the circumstances in hushed whispers.

'What's he going to do?'

'I don't like his chances of getting a vehicle to transport everyone in.'

'Not much comes along this road.'

'Do you think he'll shoot us and just take the children?'

Ted walked past us over to the utility. He kicked the front right wheel that was looking slightly askew and was now protruding out from the rest of the mangled mess of metal that had been squashed back towards the cabin. He looked intently at both the wrecked utility and the massive timber jinker's back right wheel, with the bent rim and flat tyre and said, 'We were lucky we didn't go over the edge here. You nearly pushed us over.'

Greg replied, 'A close call.'

Greg added, 'So what are you going to do now? Looks like you're stuck here.'

Ted answered, 'Easy! I will commandeer the next car that comes along, I'll be able to squeeze any number of people into it. I've used an axe before to make an air hole in a boot so people can breathe. Don't you worry. I can sort things out.'

Mmm... Nine children and six adults. Impossible! I can't quite picture that. Certainly not comfortably or safely.

It really seemed like an impossible situation. What sort of vehicle could possibly transport us all but would still suit Ted's requirements? A range of vehicles might be big enough to hold the children so he could take them away. It seemed in all probability that he would leave us blokes behind or get rid of us in some way. I was concerned that the children and I might become separated. I felt a very deep sense of responsibility. That he might end up with the children all by himself certainly did not sit well with my thinking.

'Oh Lord, help us,' I prayed.

We waited.

>>><<<

We heard the first tell-tale sounds of another vehicle approaching in the far distance. It was coming from the direction that we had been heading.

We all pricked up our ears.

A police car? A search party on the lookout for us, as the result of an early alert? It didn't sound like a truck. It was much too quiet and I couldn't hear the changing of gears. Slowly the noise became more distinct. Closer and closer. The sound ebbed and waned as the vehicle travelled around the bends in the road that followed the curves in the mountains.

Once again Ted was on full alert. We were all on full alert.

Ted began to walk to our right, past the children, towards the direction of the oncoming vehicle.

Our view of the approaching vehicle was partly obscured because we were flat on our bellies and partway around the corner. There was a considerable amount of grass and scrub between our line of sight and the next corner in the road. We watched as Ted walked slowly in that direction.

Then we saw it. Raising our heads a little, we were able to work out some detail. It looked like a Kombi Van and there appeared to be two people in it.

Ted casually approached the van at almost sixty metres from where we were lying. Presumably, he didn't want whoever was in that vehicle seeing the scene before he stopped them.

In similar fashion to the previous encounters with the drivers of the two trucks, Ted with gun well-hidden, nonchalantly approached the Kombi Van, which had stopped short with the approach of Ted. The driver wound down the window and Ted, going in closer to the open window, began to engage them in conversation, presumably stating that there had been an accident and that help was required.

The driver and passenger of the van were women. Ted pointed the gun at them, presumably once he'd decided they weren't much of a threat and told them it was a hold up.

The men and I were unable to hear the interchange but Ted grabbed the keys out of the ignition and demanded that the women get out of the van. They were also ordered to hand over or tell him where the spare keys were. Apparently, there were none. Totally mystified, and probably terrified, they were forced to sit on the left-hand side of the road, next to their vehicle.

I can only imagine what these ladies must have been thinking, but bless them, they stayed in full control of their emotions and simply did what they were instructed to do.

Ted now had a vehicle that he could transport us all in. He was back in business.

This Kombi was decked out as a camper van. It was mustard-coloured with a white roof and trims. It had a spare tyre protruding out the front, attached to the bull bar. The two women were from Melbourne, travelling around Gippsland on holidays and were 'lucky' enough to come along at just the right time.

Of all the vehicles to come around the bend, I couldn't believe it was a Kombi Van. For Ted, this was possibly the best vehicle imaginable. Except for an empty mini bus, I couldn't think of anything else close to being suitable for transporting seventeen people.

Did I want things to work out?

For Ted? No.

For the rest of us? Yes.

For things to work out for us at this point though, at one level we needed things to work out for Ted.

The timing and the direction of this van was amazingly providential. What would have happened if the Kombi had come from the other direction? The road was impassable.

We could have been waiting for ages for something remotely suitable. What would have happened if more trucks and timber jinkers had come along with more drivers and passengers? What if a normal sedan car had arrived with another two people in it? Ted reckoned he could have smashed an air-hole in a sedan's boot with the axe, so he could put bodies in there. I wasn't too sure how he could execute that plan. I hate to think what might have been if that had eventuated. Bodies crammed in a boot suffocating to death!

I figured that if almost any other kind of vehicle had come along, if Ted couldn't fit us all in, then someone, or several of us, would be left behind, possibly dead. The Kombi Van meant that the children and I stayed together and better yet, I had these guys as companions and as safety valves.

It wasn't just a perfect vehicle for the job though, we also acquired two perfect angels. Those women were an absolute God-send, I was soon to discover.

Their names: Joy Edward and Muriel Deipenau.

Ted went to the children and ushered them over to the left side of the van to join the ladies who were seated between the van and the steep embankment.

Ted then immediately headed in our direction.

A bond between the ladies and the children began. The love and care they gave the children from the moment of their meeting was stunning. Although I was unable to hear or see properly, greetings, hugs and introductions were made along with a few tears. A special relationship between the children and these women started to grow.

Ted approached me and the men with gun in hand.

I heard David just to my left whisper something to Robin, about jumping him. Robin replied with a comment to do with the time needing to be right.

I stated, 'We've got to be careful... for the kids.'

Ted came upon us quickly. He stood in front of us and ordered, 'Okay blokes. Flat on your bellies. Arms out! Up above your heads.'

We obeyed.

He then moved to where the chain was padlocked to the rear of the truck. He released the padlock, letting the chain fall to the ground. He put the padlock and key back in his pocket.

Threats and warnings again were made, not to set a foot out of place.

'Don't try anything stupid any of you. I've got the gun and I'm prepared to use it.'

I didn't doubt it.

'Now stand up and walk towards the van. One behind the other.'

Led by Greg and followed by Ian and me, with David and Robin at the rear, we headed towards our new mode of transport.

It must have been a weird sight to see five men manacled together with a dog chain, walking behind each other, all chained in one line, on a road in the Gippsland ranges, overseen by a man wielding a small handgun.

We clinked our way over to the back of the van, one behind the other, followed by our captor with the revolver pointed at our backs. The end of the chain dragged along in the gravel behind Robin. It scraped and jingled on the gravel road. Ted trailed behind at some distance watching us very closely.

Why didn't five men, four of whom were rugged 'truckies', and all of whom had only one of their hands fastened to a chain, overpower this one man and his revolver at this point? Surely this was the perfect opportunity. The children were removed, over at the Kombi with the women, a good distance away, not in the firing line of the gun. Why didn't we all jump him?

Ted was very shrewd throughout, particularly when it came to dealing with five men. He generally stood back with revolver in hand, giving himself enough distance to shoot any of us who may have decided to try to tackle him. Up to this point, each time there had been a padlock to be locked or unlocked there was always the order to put our hands and arms out straight. Along with the added threats and warnings, the gun in hand had always pointed in our direction or was carefully placed in his front right pocket, at the ready. He was undoubtedly well practiced in what it meant to be a prisoner.

We approached the van. Joy, Muriel and the children were still getting acquainted. There was pleasant chatter between them. The children had smiles on their faces and looked considerably cheerier than I had seen them look since Ted had appeared in our school room.

I estimated the women to be in their late forties or early fifties. Joy, the owner of the van, was of medium height, fair in complexion and wearing glasses. Muriel was slightly taller, slimmer in build, with dark hair and dark glasses.

The women were giving the children their full attention. They gave us passing glances with quizzical looks on their faces as Ted ushered us towards them. They must have been wondering what in the heck they had driven into. A leisurely holiday drive one minute and a bizarre kidnapping situation the next. It must have been a massive shock and totally unbelievable. Upon observing the ladies at this point though, I saw no sign of shock on their part, just puzzled looks while they loved these needy children who were going through a hellish experience. Kay and Bernie were both hanging onto Joy's and Muriel's hands. Leanne and Lucy were talking with Muriel about something. The children were openly 'lapping it up' and enjoying the kindness.

The women and children were curtly ordered to get in the van through the side sliding door, near where they were mingling, as quickly as possible. Ted was in a hurry. Amongst other things, he must have been concerned about the possibility of more vehicles arriving on the scene.

They piled in. The women and six girls in the back. The three boys in the front.

Then we five men were instructed to climb in the back of the van also, but it was already full.

Ted was standing at the front of the van, some distance from me and the other men. He moved around to the driver's door and looked in through the window.

He said to Joy, Muriel and the girls, 'Squash up! Make room. We need to fit five more people in.'

Once again, they followed the order. The ladies helped organise the girls. Some moved to the floor. Jill sat on Maggie's knee. All squashed in, making room for the men.

We then began to clamber in. First Greg and Ian, then me followed by David and Robin, all linked with the chain.

Somehow, we were all able to squeeze in. Some were sitting on a narrow bench seat that ran along the left-side of the van. Three of us were on the bench seat on the front right. Others were sitting with knees up around their chins on the floor. A top bunk bed on the back right of the van had someone lying in it, very close to the roof with very little room to move. All were sharing the limited space jammed up next to others.

It was like sardines in a can. Six men, two women and nine children squashed into that one small camper van. Seventeen people. Crazy stuff!

Once we were all in the back, Ted ordered Robin, who was closest to him, to padlock the end of the chain to a handle hold that was positioned just inside the sliding door, on the roof of the van. Ted didn't want any of the blokes to make a run for it. The rest of us, from our various seating positions watched and wondered how Robin would react, with Ted being so close. Ted was holding the gun in his right hand pointing it straight at Robin's head. With his left hand, he threw Robin an unlocked padlock and watched Robin intently, still holding the gun.

We all wondered if Robin might try something.

Robin caught the padlock. Ted continued to point the gun at Robin's head.

Ted threatened, 'Don't try anything heroic, smart boy. You know I'll shoot. Just do what I say and no one will get hurt. I'm watching very closely and I can see if you do it correctly. I need to hear the lock click into place.'

Robin slowly leaned down and picked up the end of the chain and threaded it through the hand hold. He then placed the padlock through two links securing them to the handle. We all heard the lock click. We were now chained to the van.

I was to find out much later that it was at this moment, more than any other, that Robin seriously considered going for the gun. However, being joined to his brother by a chain and then that same chain being joined to the rest of us, Robin thought that perhaps the room he had to move in may have been seriously hampered and therefore the time was not right.

I imagine that all the different possibilities and the varying outcomes from Robin's actions would have played out in his mind over the years. Like me, there would have been the cold sweats, the adrenaline rushes and palpitations.

Ted didn't seem to mind that the children and women were not tied up. Besides the lack of materials to secure everyone, I think he reasoned that he wasn't likely to be attacked by any of them and that there was little point in any of them running off. Running away seemed out of the question for a number of reasons. Firstly, he had a gun and was evidently in charge and the kids and women weren't about to risk their lives. Secondly, we were in the most remote and isolated place imaginable, so where would they run to? And thirdly, there was more security in staying with the group than in going it alone. The women had already begun to take some responsibility of caring for the children which, I suspect, also added to his sense that they weren't likely to run off.

Having made sure all his prisoners were in the vehicle, Ted got in himself. With van keys in hand, he started sorting through the various key options. He tried one in the ignition, then another, but none worked.

Slightly embarrassed, he had to revert to asking Joy, 'Which key operates this machine?'

Joy obliged and directed him to the correct key.

It was one of those moments! Although he was in control as our captor, ironically, he was reduced to needing Joy to help him find the right key.

She then added, 'Would you like me to drive it too?'

'Not likely! You would drive us to the nearest police station,' Ted answered.

He then started up the van.

THE GRAND RIDGE ROAD: 2.30PM

Once Ted had started the Kombi he had to turn the vehicle around, which was not an easy task on such a narrow road. He reversed about thirty metres to where the road was slightly wider. It then took something like a five-point turn to turn around. And he had to venture so close to that veritable cliff edge to execute the manoeuvre. Everyone held their breath each time the nose of the van inched towards the precipice. We all breathed a sigh of relief as he completed the 180-degree turn.

Off we set again, driving at a reckless speed. We were travelling in the direction that we had always been heading, which was where the ladies had come from. The road continued to be rough and rugged, windy and undulating.

Be careful, man! You've only just escaped from one accident. Now you're in a new vehicle that you've never driven before, driving in extremely difficult conditions and you have my students on board. Slow down!

As good as this vehicle was, it was obvious that we were loaded up far beyond its capacity. I could sense the difficulty Ted found in steering and keeping the van steady on the road with the extra weight. The van seemed to have a rolling movement each time he had to steer around bends and corners. Braking was also a real issue: it took much longer to slow down. The level of risk he was taking was enormous. The combined factors of high speed, overloading, hilly terrain, sharp bends in the road and the rough surface meant extremely high levels of danger.

*Above and Left:
Safe at Sale Police
Station.*

Photos Courtesy of
Victoria Police Museum.

*Above: Mr Thompson
with students and Rob.*

*Left: Mr Thompson
at Press Conference.*

At Sale — relieved but dishevelled.
Photo Courtesy The Sun News-Pictorial.

Students and Rob at Sale.
Photo Courtesy Joy Edward.

Students and Rob at Sale.
Photo Courtesy The Sun News-Pictorial.

*Roadside scene
photos immediately
after the rescue.*
Photos Courtesy
Joy Edward.

*Left: Greg and
Robin.*

Above: Truckies.

Left: Chained.

Immediately after the rescue.

Plain clothes police.

*Above: 40 Year Reunion. From
back left: Ray Argento, Brett
Fisher, Rob Hunter, Leonie Smith,
Danny Forrester. From front left:
Josephine Cue, Robin Smith,
Maree McFarlane.*

*Below: 40 Year Reunion. Rob
with his hero Robin Smith.*

Photos Courtesy Roy Fisher.

*Above: Researching
at Police Museum.*
Photo Courtesy John D Pallot.

Education Department book celebration.

Above: From left: Danny Forrester, Maree McFarlane, Ray Argento, Rob Hunter, Karina Finch, Joy Butters (Edward), Leonie Smith, Robin Smith, Ian Webber, Laurene McKenzie, Rohan McKenzie.

Below: Rob and Robin with Regional Director Jeanette Nagorcka.

Photos courtesy Smokey Oscar.

Right: David Thompson (son of Lindsay Thompson) and Rob.

Below: Jennifer Riley (daughter of Mick Miller) and Rob.

Right: Joy Butters (Edward) with Maree McFarlane.

Below: Rob and Judi Hunter family.

Ted had his window down. The noise of the vehicle driving over the rough gravel road was loud.

I'm sure all of us were thinking about the possibility of gaining the attention of a passing car. Could we alert someone to what was happening to us? Could we wave someone down? Not that there was a hint of any other vehicles being around at this point.

Ted too had the possibility on his mind. A warning was issued.

'Anyone who tries to do something smart like waving down someone, look out! I've got the gun and I'll shoot you!'

The boys in the front seat were ordered to duck their heads whenever a car approached.

I wondered how much fuel was in the van. By moving slightly to my right, from my position to the back left of Ted, I could just make out some of the details on the dashboard in front of him. The petrol tank was around three quarters full. Enough fuel to drive for some four hours or more, I guessed. I assumed that was an ample supply to get us to wherever we were going.

For the first time that day, I was able to see where we were going and how Ted was handling the van, and I had a much better feel for the whole situation. There was such a marked contrast between this drive and the first leg of my journey. Now, I had company and support. The children were within my reach. I was in a seated position and not facing backwards. I could see. My bonds were significantly less constricting than they previously were and I wasn't feeling car sick.

However, I was still very worried about our situation. The children's lives continued to be in serious danger. I was also hungry, thirsty, dirty and smelly.

We continued travelling very fast. Robin warned us in the back that there was a high likelihood of encountering more logging trucks. The thought of meeting another one on the many corners that we were speeding around was a serious worry.

Ted continued on, apparently with little thought of such dangers.

We were travelling through very rugged country covered in thick bush. The road wound around very steep hills. There were cuttings in the side of the surrounding hills that had been engineered by local shires, mostly for logging trucks and vehicles associated with forestry, it seemed. It was beautiful country. Under normal circumstances I would have thoroughly enjoyed the freshness and grandeur of the Gippsland bush.

Majestic gum trees were everywhere. They were beautiful. The bark was peeling off and hanging from branches and forks in the trees, swaying in the breeze. Where the bark had peeled, new clean and fresh trunk was exposed with intriguing light grey patterns. The undergrowth was thick, taller than a man. There were twisted vines and a variety of smaller bushy trees. All the while there were the tree ferns scattered along the way. However, this bush had now become the passage to our destination, where we were to be held hostage.

Quiet conversations took place in the back of the van obscured from Ted by the constant noise of the vehicle on the gravel road.

I greeted each of the women. We exchanged names and made comments about the ludicrousness of the situation. Interspersed by conversations with the children, the women asked questions of me and the other guys. They wanted to know where we were from and how he had kidnapped us. Muriel asked why I hadn't locked the door of the school so he couldn't get in. I tried to explain the situation of children going outside for recess and being rounded up and ordered back in. I'm not sure that she understood. They wanted to know what time we had left the school and if any of the parents were likely to visit the school during the day and how the accident happened. I explained about the ransom letter that had been posted.

The children did their share of the talking, answering as many questions as I did.

I spoke very briefly with each of the children. Maggie, Lucy and Jill explained how the trip in the back of the utility had been.

'Bernie and Dale vomited heaps,' Lucy said.

'Yeah! Bernie's vomit ended up in my hair,' complained Leanne.

I asked Bernie how she was feeling now, to which she replied that being able to get out of the utility and get some fresh air had made a big difference.

Maggie said, 'Ron hit his head really hard at the accident and ended up with a blood-nose.'

Leanne reported that Dale's vomit had partly gone over Russell's arm.

Jill said, 'Kay got cut by the glass when Ted smashed the window in.'

I asked Kay to show me the cut. It was a relatively small cut on the side of her leg which I didn't think would cause too much trouble. Joy agreed with me and said that she would put a band aid on it once we got to our destination, if Ted would let her.

I leant over the front and spoke briefly to each of the boys. Dale said he was fine now. I checked on Ron, asking him how his blood nose was, to which he gave me a little smile and said he was okay. I could see the signs of dried blood around his face. I asked Russell how he was. He responded with a wry smile. The boys mostly kept their eyes on the road, not saying much. They appeared to be okay in the front with Ted. Each time a vehicle of any sort approached they ducked their heads as requested. I felt unable to speak to them much, since they were beside Ted.

Various other details were shared with the girls in the back. One of the girls mentioned how we had been through Mirboo North and had gone right past the police station and that we had stopped in Mirboo North to post a letter. This was news to me. I still had absolutely no idea where we were, but it seemed like too much of a coincidence that we had stopped at my new home town.

Each of the children looked rather dishevelled and unruly. Some had traces of vomit down their clothes. Some bloodied. All dusty and dirty. Most of their hair was ruffled and messy. Faces looked strained and grubby. It was like they had been out bush for a week. They were all in need of their parents' caring touch and something to eat and drink.

Bernie was sitting close to Joy and enjoying her company, chatting quietly in little bursts from time to time. Leanne was chatting with Kay, showing sisterly concern. Maggie, Lucy and Jill were sitting closely together keeping each other company.

'Good on you girls,' I said. 'Thank you for looking after each other. Well done!'

One of the ladies whispered to me, 'You know who this bloke is don't you?'

'No,' I replied.

'I think he's Eastwood. He did this before at Faraday, near Bendigo. He had a friend who did it with him. He's escaped from prison.'

My mind ticked over. *Faraday. It was all over the news years ago. Mary Gibbs and her six children locked up in a van.*

>><<<

This 'Ted' was Edwin John Eastwood, the Faraday kidnapper of 1972.

In October of 1972, Edwin John Eastwood, with his accomplice Robert Boland, kidnapped Mary Gibbs and her six children from their school at Faraday, near Bendigo in Central Victoria. Under heroic circumstances, Mary Gibbs was able to free herself and her six students, to escape the captivity of the van that they were being held in and run to safety. Eastwood and Boland were subsequently caught and imprisoned.

But on December 16, 1976 (about the same time that I received my appointment to Wooreen) Eastwood escaped from the Geelong Training Prison where he was being held. A police report recorded the spate of crime that followed:

- December 16, Eastwood stole a Holden utility from Richmond Street, East Geelong.
- January 2, 1977, Eastwood stole number plates from a Grey Cortina in Patterson Road, Bentleigh.
- January 26, Eastwood stole a Holden Sedan from William Street, Brighton.
- February 1, Eastwood stole a white Holden Utility from Railway Road, Trafalgar (when this vehicle was later recovered in Frankston it was missing a certain tarpaulin).

- February 2, Eastwood stole a grey Dodge one-ton utility containing a large amount of carpentry tools from Santa Barbara Drive, Frankston.
- February 8, Eastwood broke into the Boolarra General Store in Mid Gippsland and stole provisions.
- In the early hours of February 14 Eastwood returned to the Boolarra General Store and stole forty-eight cartons of milk – these were the drinks for his intended captives for his next kidnapping feat which he was to implement that day; a near duplicate of his previous evil deed.

>>><<<

It was all beginning to make some degree of sense.

So, this is the same bloke as back then. He's an escapee. Just as we guessed. The story he told me earlier, before the accident, about reading of the Faraday kidnapping in the paper was bull dust. He did it! And Bernie's question in the classroom asking whether he had done this before was right on the money.

How in the heck were we going to get out of this? There didn't seem to be any possibilities for me to do anything.

I was seated in the forward part of the back of the van on a cushioned seat, facing sideways. Complete luxury compared to my previous travel. I had a certain amount of space but I was still jammed up against one of the men from the trucks. It was Ian Webber. No one looked comfortable, Ian as little as anyone else. He also had to put up with the stink of my vomit hanging around, though he never complained.

Ian and I chatted briefly. He had hitched a ride with Greg that morning because he enjoyed the company and the truck scene. He told me that he hadn't enjoyed school much, had finished school the year before and was now looking for a job.

'Where are we?' I asked him.

He mentioned various places. The only part I remember was, 'near Carrajung and not far from Won Wron.' This meant absolutely nothing to me. I was conscious that we were heading in a general easterly direction, the sun being mostly behind us. Sometimes we were going in more northerly and sometimes southerly directions.

It seemed now that Eastwood wasn't too sure of where he was going. He did one U-turn. Then he had to reverse when he missed a turn. He kept closely scrutinising all the road signs, although they were few and far between.

On we drove. Still driving much too fast over rough, bumpy and often pot-holed roads. All unsealed. Steep descents. Steep inclines. Sharp and not so sharp bends. A few intersections. Whenever we passed other vehicles, Eastwood reminded the children in the front to duck their heads and he gave a small friendly wave. He wore a peaked cap now, the modified football beanie not having been seen since the first minutes in the school. Sunglasses were over his eyes helping to obscure any obvious features from passing vehicles that may have given his identity away.

After a while we found ourselves on a flatter road in a more level terrain. We were leaving the Strzelecki Ranges behind us and as I found out later, heading to the plains of South-East Gippsland around Woodside and Yarram.

We were now passing the occasional farm. The roads were better made and less windy. There were some sealed stretches of road and there was quite a bit more traffic. We saw farmers on tractors and farm bikes working their land.

Still on we drove. About two hours of painstaking travel. I thought, *how much further do we have to go? How much more can these children put up with? How much more can I put up with?* Did anyone complain? Hardly.

At some stage, the ladies suggested that they could pour a drink.

Oh! Yes, please. I really need that!

My mouth and throat were so dry.

They apologised for their supplies being low and hence not having a lot to go around.

It was decided that I should ask Eastwood for permission for the ladies to pour a drink out of their supplies.

'Excuse me Ted,' I called into the front. 'Do you mind if the ladies pour a drink for the children?'

Thankfully, he nodded and said that would be fine.

Joy poured water from their polystyrene drink container. We all shared meagre rations, about half a cup of water each. There were two cups. We shared. First the children and then the adults.

Oh, that drink! I swished it around in my mouth. Fresh clean water rinsing my mouth and then down my throat. So good! I would have loved some more, but it wasn't on offer.

Eastwood was following a map. He had it sitting in front of him on the steering wheel. Now and again he would slow down to study it more closely. Right here. Left there.

At a corner, he stopped and studied the map carefully.

It became obvious that he had gotten himself lost. Looking intently at the map. Studying the signposts. Looking for another road. Eastwood appeared perplexed. Muttering under his breath he turned around, backtracking in search of some missing road. He was lost! We were all lost!

Although my seat was cushioned, facing sideways and jammed in with little leg room, the comfort level was not high. Everyone was clearly uncomfortable and we'd all certainly had enough.

'Where are we going?'

'How much further do we have to go?'

'How long before we get there?'

The children were beginning to ask. The questions were aimed at me and the ladies mainly. Eastwood was also asked by us and the children.

'Not far now,' was the standard response.

We backtracked a long way. He couldn't find the particular road that he was looking for.

This drive seemed to go on forever.

It must have been well over two and a half hours of driving from English's Corner. On and on it went. We were all totally sick of it; at the end of our tethers. Cramped, tired, thirsty, hungry and scared for our lives, we were all on the edge of losing our minds.

I wondered what was happening back at school. I guessed that it was about 4.30pm. Action would have kicked in, I suspected. Parents would be alarmed. Police would have been called. People would be searching. But how long before they would find us in far off East Gippsland, or wherever we were?

In fact, we weren't in far off East Gippsland. Far from it. It just felt like it. I found out later that we were not too far from Yarram, the major town in the eastern part of South Gippsland.

For goodness sake! Are we ever going to stop?

Then we came to another sealed road. A signpost read, 'Woodside 8km'. The other men and the ladies were very interested. It meant very little to me.

Eastwood became more confident with his whereabouts and it was clear that in his mind at least we weren't lost. We had turned onto a main road which the truck drivers in hushed voices explained to me was the South Gippsland Highway. We were somewhere between Woodside and Darriman in South-East Gippsland. I didn't fully realise at the time but Robin and Greg knew exactly where we were throughout the trip. They'd been driving on these roads for years. On that day and the days prior they had been picking up logs from Womerah in the Tarra Valley hauling them along the Grand Ridge Road to the mill at Boolarra. In retrospect, it is comical to think that Eastwood had been lost and yet these two locals who knew the roads like the back of their hands were remaining silent, as captives in the back.

It surprised me that having been in such secluded and out-of-the-way places all day that we would find ourselves on a major highway. It was a fully sealed bitumen road with what appeared to me to be beautiful clear white lines, so different to anything I had seen all day. I enjoyed a brief sense of civilisation. The sides of the road were adorned with white posts and there were regular markings indicating the distance to the nearest large town which I guessed to be Sale. It was in such contrast to the roads that we had traversed all day.

Perhaps there was a chance of a police car randomly wanting to check this over-loaded Kombi.

We saw no such police car.

Then off this highway Eastwood saw on our left, heading back in a westerly direction, a very minor, gravel road, which he seemed very interested in. It was sign-posted Boundary Road. It seemed like we were going to turn into it, however at the last minute he became highly concerned about an approaching vehicle. He didn't want them seeing us turn into that particular road. I wondered how any vehicle going at full speed could possibly be interested in us, but plainly Eastwood was taking no chances.

Slowing down to a crawl, we continued on for one to two hundred metres past Boundary Road. He waited until he was certain there were no other vehicles in sight, quickly performed a U-turn, and hastily drove back to the same little road and darted into it.

There was a farm house on the opposite side of the main road. It was a little further north of Boundary Road. I only vaguely noticed this house at the time but it would later be of some significance to our plight.

Off we drove again, along the minor road. Once again it was a bumpy, dusty road. This one had quite a sandy aspect to it. We continued to bounce along, bumping and brushing up against each other. The children on the floor must have been unbelievably uncomfortable. Their butts must have hurt more than mine. We'd been gone from the school some six hours at this point I reckoned.

It seemed interminable!

We came to an intersection of rough unmade roads going off in varying directions. There were some hard-to-read sign-posts. One sign-post said Mile Road. We veered left and then on we went, straight again. It seemed to me that we'd been along so many roads and through so many intersections all day, these were just more of the same.

Despite my discomfort and concerns, I had a sense that the accident, although potentially fatal, had become the children's and my friend. It meant that I wasn't doing this alone, which I was particularly thankful for. I felt like the four chained up guys were now my best buddies and the two women were like our mothers. I was also thankful that I wasn't still blind-folded, kneeling or slumped on the floor of Eastwood's utility like I would have been if we hadn't run into Robin and David in their timber jinker. Similarly, the children would have still been jammed in the back of the dusty vehicle accompanied by their vomit, the warm cartons of milk and the remains of their lunches. Along with those sufferings, our dehydrations would have made it even more overwhelming.

We were now in fairly flat country, with only gentle rises and dips. The dirt at the side of the road was a sandier soil than normal, as was the road itself. There were no steep or grand hills like we had driven through for most of the day and nor was the vegetation as thick as it had been in the ranges. The trees here were smaller and considerably sparser. These trees had a much darker and untidy trunk, more like an iron bark tree, unlike the picturesque blue gums that we'd constantly passed by earlier. Where the dark bark had fallen away, there was left a lighter blotchy grey coloured surface. They weren't particularly attrac-tive. The undergrowth likewise wasn't as heavy. It was mostly a fine, scrubby plant, a melaleuca or wattle perhaps. In places, it was taller than a man but mostly it was around chest height. The grass, although green and prevalent, was a little tuftier and drier looking.

Eastwood knew where he was going.

'We're almost there,' he said. 'Five minutes.'

Thank goodness! About time!

I reckon that was everyone's thought.

I wondered what our destination was to be like. *Will there be a building? A shelter of some sort? A tent?*

After about eight to ten kilometres along this road we turned off to the right onto a tiny bush track. We drove along this rough track for about four hundred metres when we came to a fork. We veered left. This part of the fork that branched off to the left was far narrower and the surface noticeably rougher than the right fork, with significant erosion where the rain had washed away much of the sandy soil. In places this track was hardly even a track as it was almost entirely covered over by the small melaleuca or wattle trees and scrub. There wasn't nearly enough room for a vehicle. Even as a walking track, a person would have had to brush past the foliage. However, Eastwood managed to squeeze our vehicle through these small spaces, brushing up hard against the shrubbery. He had obviously been this way before. We continued very slowly over the very rough track for a further one to two hundred metres.

Even though we'd been in remote isolated locations all day, this was worse. This was even more secluded and lonely. It was removed from any sense of human habitation. It seemed to me that this was so out-of- the-way that no one would ever find us or stumble upon us.

Then what was left of a track seemed to totally disappear.

We found ourselves in a clearing. It looked like a camping spot, of sorts, all prepared for Ted's captives.

PART THREE

CAMP SITE: 5.00PM

A large tree stood in the middle of the clearing. The space, eight to ten metres or more in each direction from the central tree, was void of any other large trees, particularly to the west side, where there was close to fifteen metres of clearing before the bush again merged into a thick cover of trees. Some of the knee-high grass and scrubby plants all around had been trampled and driven over, which made the clearing look camp-like and suggested that Eastwood had been camping here himself for some time. There was a large pile of something, covered over with an outstretched tarpaulin at the foot of the tree. We soon discovered that this pile was in fact the provisions intended to cater for the teacher and children for days on end.

How will anyone ever find us in a place like this?

Eastwood drove the van into this partly open area. He then reversed back into the left-hand side of our entry point, backing the rear of the van into the wooded edge of the clearing, underneath the cover of some trees.

He ordered us to stay where we were, while he climbed out.

Eastwood set about removing the five men first. With the gun in his hand he opened the sliding door. Standing well back he stated, 'Okay. You five fellas out! Don't try anything smart.'

This was a tricky manoeuvre for Eastwood for a variety of reasons. Robin and David Smith were very close to the door of the vehicle, well within reach of Eastwood as he opened the sliding door. He was on full alert for anything shifty.

Instead of undoing the chain that was padlocked to the roof of the van first, Eastwood stood well back with the gun pointed at us and told the men to climb out.

It was awkward. We were still tied together by a chain and since we had been sitting on numb bums in extremely uncomfortable and confined positions for about three hours, we had to carefully and gradually unwind ourselves and stretch out.

We slowly worked our way out on to the earth, closely watched by Eastwood, with the gun in hand.

Despite the circumstances, particularly the constant gun threats, it was a very good feeling to be able to stand on solid ground and straighten my body out, even if it was only for a few seconds.

Eastwood made us all kneel on the ground with our hands on our heads facing away from the van and as far away as the chain would reach from its secured state to the handle in the van. We were all in a line with Greg in the lead and Robin at the rear. Robin was only a metre or two from the van. Once we were all kneeling with our hands on our heads Eastwood walked behind us, back over to the door of the van. Since Robin was closest to the van, I guessed that Eastwood would have been wary of his close proximity.

He said, 'No funny business, Singlet. I'm watching you.'

Placing the gun in his front right pocket, Eastwood then fossicked around in his left trouser pocket for the key to undo the padlock. Finding the correct key, he unlocked the padlock from the roof of the van and allowed the end of the chain to drop to the ground.

We were instructed to stand and walk to the tree. Once again, the chain gang of five moved along, joined at the wrist.

The end of the chain dragged along in the grass and scrub behind us, accompanied by our feet crunching and cracking on the dead leaves and sticks.

The children and women, watching from the van, must have wondered how on earth such bizarre things could really be happening.

Once at the tree he ordered us all to lie flat on our bellies, in a semi-circle around the north side of the tree, again with our hands and arms stretched out above our heads, faces centimetres from the ground, while he secured the chain around the tree. The ground was hard, covered with thick, long tufty grass and a variety of small plants. There were a lot of dead leaves, sticks, small branches and dead grass mixed with the sandy soil. I breathed the strong scent of the plant life and the dry ground. This was somewhat better than the last time we had been flat on our faces. The tree itself was very large. The trunk would have been about one and a half metres in diameter. There were black burnt patches around it, signs of a fire from some time ago. There was a gentle slope from where I lay leading up to the base of the tree: a buildup of debris and compost over many years.

Eastwood grabbed the two ends of the chain and padlocked them around the other side of the tree. Having secured the chain around the tree, we were free to move our hands and arms, back level with our shoulders.

Eastwood said, 'Okay fellas, you can move again now. You're not going very far with that tree though.'

He laughed. He thought it was funny. We didn't.

He added, 'Don't forget who's got the power here.'

Five men tied around a tree in the middle of nowhere. Having the chain tied around my wrist and joined to Ian and

David on either side, about one metre apart, didn't leave much room for movement.

Next came Joy, Muriel and the children. They remained untied and able to move freely, in direct contrast to the men. Eastwood walked behind them with little concern of any rebellion. There was a discussion between Eastwood and the ladies about chaining them up. He reasoned with them and said that if they cooperated fully he wouldn't worry about chaining them. They agreed that they would give him no trouble. Along with the children they were told to sit under the tree, but away from the men. We were on the north side of the tree, while they spread out on the south side, approximately ten metres away from us. The tree trunk partly obscured my vision of them. They were in a position where the ground sloped down into a small depression. The children continued looking to these ladies for comfort and direction. Bernie and Kay in particular were still enjoying the close contact.

At the foot of the tree on the south side lay the pile of supplies underneath the tarpaulin. Eastwood hadn't bargained on picking up six extra adults. I wondered how he was going to provide for all seventeen people, for who knew how long?

Eastwood first pulled the tarpaulin off the pile. He instructed the women to share the blankets around. With the tarpaulin in hand, he headed over to the van.

The women gave some of the blankets to the children to sit on. Likewise, there were some more blankets that they handed to the men to lie on. Some of the cushions and bedding from the van were later added to the collection.

Eastwood carefully laid the tarpaulin over the van, along with some tree branches to obscure its presence from the air. He must have been acutely aware of the certain pursuit of police and the possibility of stray eyes seeing our whereabouts.

All of the children wanted to go to the toilet. Most of us had been hanging on all day.

Eastwood had dug a hole for the 'number twos' some distance away on the west side of the clearing. The children, one by one, were allowed to go and relieve themselves, partly supervised by the ladies but overseen from a distance of about twenty or more metres by Eastwood.

I wondered how he would allow me and the other men to relieve ourselves. At that moment, I still didn't need to go to the toilet, having had so little to drink all day. Man! I was thirsty though.

Once all the children and women had relieved themselves, our kidnapper gave the ladies the job of distributing the meagre rations of water, milk and tinned ham.

Joy worked on sharing the ham around. She pulled the lid off one of the tins. With it still in the tin, Joy cut some slices of the soft rubbery mixture with a knife that Eastwood supplied her with. She then offered pieces to the children, levering slices out with the knife. A full tin was demolished before it made it to the men. Another was opened. Once again Joy distributed the contents. This time the men and I were first to be served.

'Are you guys okay?' she asked.

'We're fine,' we answered.

I said, 'Thanks for looking after the children.'

Joy responded, 'Poor little honeys! What a horrible thing for them to have to go through. They're doing so well though.'

I continued to have a deep sense of appreciation for her and Muriel's care of the children.

I'd had this particular ham many times at home and I quite liked it. As a child, I thought it was a delicacy. It came in a predominately blue coloured, egg shaped tin. Some people may have referred to it as 'spam'. This may have been partly true, but in my opinion, it was of a significantly higher quality than the 'spam hams' that came in the smaller and more oval shaped tins.

One of the things I had always liked about this sort of ham was the thin ring of jelly that was usually around the outside of it. And this ham had that ring of jelly. I was ready and waiting for my turn to have a portion.

The other men and I were in sitting positions now. Joy levered out a slice with her knife and with very grubby fingers I took a piece and savored the lovely taste in my mouth.

Yes! Just like I'd enjoyed at home. Very nice!

Even though I was in a dire situation and so much seemed to be against me, I have to admit that I thoroughly enjoyed eating my piece of ham that day.

Eastwood's water seemed to be in scarce supply, so water from the van was used as well. Muriel served everyone a cup full which was greatly appreciated. I would have loved some more but one cup of water each was the ration. Muriel and Joy had already stated that their supply of water was limited. Water was obviously a scarce commodity.

There was a large number of cigarette cartons in Eastwood's supplies. Enough for an army I thought. One whole carton was passed around. Just one packet was opened and shared between us. A few of the guys smoked. Ian had a cigarette lighter. I occasionally indulged in a smoke so I too had a couple of cigarettes over the course of the evening, although I waited until it was dark as I wasn't prepared to smoke in front of the children. It helped pass the time.

Greg asked Eastwood where he had got the smokes from. 'I stole them!' he boasted. We assumed that everything was stolen, which proved to be the case.

There was also a whole stack of family size blocks of chocolate in the supplies. He gave Lucy half a dozen of these blocks and suggested that she might like to share them around. Lucy, a very eager and cheerful child who was always wanting to help, was in her element.

Lucy worked her way around all the children and the women and then came by each of the men to offer us some of the cubes of chocolate that she had carefully broken up. Smiles were traded between her and me.

Taking a few pieces of chocolate, I asked quietly, 'Are you okay? Has Kay's cut been attended to? How are the bruises?'

Lucy's response was brief and all in the positive. A band aid had been applied to Kay's cut.

Having had something to eat and drink, some of the men also needed to take a trip to the makeshift toilet to relieve themselves.

Greg, two to my right, initiated the move.

First, he asked me and Ian if we needed to go to the toilet.

Ian said he did. I didn't have a desperate urge but thought it would be a good opportunity to stretch out and that it was best to go when and if the others were going, so I said yes also.

Greg called out to Eastwood who was standing up not far away, smoking a cigarette, 'Hey Ted! Can we go to the toilet please?'

Eastwood agreed. After a few more draws on his cigarette, he stubbed it out and headed towards us.

Approaching five men that he was holding captive was a risky business. After all, we were five men that would have loved to have jumped him and he knew it. He didn't come very close at all. From a distance of approximately three to four metres, he asked Greg what the number on his lock was. Once identified, Eastwood found the corresponding key and then threw it to Greg, for him to undo his own lock. Having undone the lock, Greg was told to leave the lock undone next to the chain and throw the key back to Eastwood, who put it back in his pocket. This ensured that Eastwood didn't need to get too close to any of us.

He then escorted Greg to the general area of the toilet, about twenty-five metres to the west. Eastwood followed about eight metres behind with gun in hand.

Once Greg had completed his task he walked back to his spot at the end of the line and proceeded to relock the chain around his wrist, all closely scrutinised by Eastwood.

Eastwood said, 'Loop the chain tightly around your wrist and put the lock back through the links. Make sure it's tight! I can see how tight you do it. No funny business or I'll shoot your hand off! I need to hear the lock click back into place.'

Greg complied.

Once Greg was secured, Eastwood moved his attention to Ian, where the same procedure was followed.

When it was my turn, like the two before me, Eastwood threw me the key. I undid my lock and threw the key back to Eastwood. I got to my feet and walked towards the toilet area, escorted at a distance by our captor.

Although I needed to empty my bladder, having not done so all day, I was unable to perform the task at hand, having a gunman standing behind me. I simply stood there in position with no action happening.

Damn! How embarrassing!

Mercifully, Eastwood commented that he had been in the same position on many occasions with 'Screws' standing behind him watching.

He said, 'Take your time, Teach. It'll come. We're not going anywhere in a hurry.'

Having received a little encouragement, after a little wait I was able to perform my function.

Eastwood's compassion at that moment caught me by surprise. On the one hand, he was wielding a gun in a threatening manner, but on the other hand he was showing a degree of consideration. I suppose there is good and bad in all of us.

Having completed the job, I was escorted back to the group. As with Greg and Ian before me, I securely fastened my own lock to the chain around my wrist.

David was next to me to my left. The same procedure was followed and he went off accompanied by Eastwood, to relieve himself.

Then it was Robin's turn. After he had been to the toilet, Robin did up his own lock closely watched by our captor. But Robin's survival instincts were kicking in.

Being a truck driver and often working with chains to secure loads, Robin knew that if he twisted the chain a little, getting some of the links to run at an angle rather than straight, he could create some extra length which would give him some crucial slack for a later moment. He was able to do this even with Eastwood's close observations, as he refastened his lock to the chain around his wrist.

We lay on the blankets and rested somewhat. The ground was hard and far from flat. It was not comfortable lying on front or back. Changing positions was not straight-forward as we needed to be mindful of each other's hands joined to the chain. Each time we moved we needed to keep our left arms relatively still so that we didn't pull on the other guy's wrists. So, we were only able to use our right hands and arms to support our movements. The jingling sounds of the chain were heard each time anyone moved.

I wondered how this affair would all turn out. How long would we have to stay tied to a tree? Eastwood had only small amounts of water and limited food. How was he going to feed us? How was he going to care for the children? Conscious of the fact that he was demanding a ransom, I wondered how he could possibly communicate with anyone to get it. Would he take us with him in the van, to make a phone call? Would he leave us for a short time, while he went somewhere? When would he need to make his next move? The whole of Victoria would be looking for him, the missing children, for me and the extra adults. How would he be able to move anywhere, without being seen?

I couldn't understand how he was going to carry out a plan. The only part of the plan we knew was that he had posted a letter, which included some ransom demands. The letter would take some time to get to its destination. Presumably the press would receive it later the next day.

We were aware that the presence of the women and their van was working in Eastwood's favour. The women had explained to us while we were travelling that they hadn't booked to stay at any accommodation and that they wouldn't be missed for at least two or more days. They were simply cruising around enjoying the countryside and staying wherever, slowly heading back to Melbourne. This meant that the police would have no idea what vehicle to look for. We recognised that once police found the mangled utility near English's Corner it would be a total mystery as to what sort of vehicle had taken us onwards.

We were also aware that the sight of the accident being in an easterly direction from Wooreen indicated that we were more than likely heading further east, giving police and rescue teams some important clues as to where we were possibly being held.

Eastwood had a reclining deck chair, a 'banana lounge', the plastic sort that I had used as a kid when camping and lazing about in the backyard at home. He sat back, reclining slightly, about eight to ten metres from us, easily able to observe his captives. He had a transistor radio which he turned on to a local station.

The women continued to take very good care of all the children. They talked calmly to them and listened patiently to their discourses about their families and other random stories of things they had done. Kay's loud, high-pitched voice stood out and could be easily heard over the others. She was enjoying sharing her tales. There seemed to be constant chatter between the children and the ladies. There was even laughter from various children. It was lovely listening to them and most reassuring, knowing that they were being cared for. It was almost absurd how relaxed and happy they were at this point. It seemed totally inconsistent with our real state of affairs. Eastwood did nothing to stop or dampen the happy conversations and dialogues.

In time, night set in. The radio was a constant.

It was a relatively warm and still night with very little or no breeze. A cloud cover was acting as a blanket, keeping the cool night air at bay. Spending the night in the Australian bush is a totally unique experience. The scent of the grass beneath me and the eucalypts around me dominated my sense of smells - there was now only an occasional whiff of vomit. The sounds of the night were there. The slight rustle of the trees. Animal noises in the surrounds. A possum nearby. There was the buzz of an occasional mosquito but they were hardly a problem. This was unusual in my mind, since all my summer camping experiences involved swarms of mosquitoes. With the lack of the little pests, I mused that there mustn't have been a lot of rain or any water lying around.

It wasn't an overly dark night, but the moon wasn't visibly shining either. It must have been behind the cloud cover as we were able to see the general shapes around us. The children expressed their fears of the dark, which the 'angels' were happy to discuss and help allay.

Thank you, God, for those ladies!

The women and the children discussed where they would sleep. It was suggested that the boys could sleep in the van, if Eastwood was happy with that. He agreed. Muriel and Eastwood took the boys over to the van, opened up the sliding door and the boys climbed in.

Chatter amongst the rest of the children and the ladies continued. Eastwood was involved in a lot of this dialogue. The remaining six girls and the women asked Eastwood questions. Eastwood's previous kidnapping was now openly discussed. He readily admitted that he was the Faraday kidnapper of 1972. He described the crime as 'the biggest in Australia'.

He predicted that this kidnapping, however, was going to be bigger than Faraday and that news of it would spread around the world. Encounters with police were discussed. Eastwood bragged that if he got caught by police he would shoot it out with them; he wouldn't be going down alone, he would shoot some of them too.

We all listened to these conversations, catching some sort of an understanding of his grandiose thinking and twisted mind.

Also discussed was the intended impact of the ransom letter, along with the problems and shortcomings from Eastwood's point of view of the State and Commonwealth Governments, Prime Minister Malcolm Fraser and the Victorian Acting Premier and Education Minister, Mr. Lindsay Thompson. He expressed his keen interest in how Mr. Thompson would react to this kidnapping situation, reaffirming his dislike for him.

Regarding Malcolm Fraser, Eastwood said, 'I'd love to get my hands on him. I'd show him a thing or two. He's a very weak Prime Minister.'

He added, 'And if Fraser and the government doesn't do a good job of securing your safety from this kidnapping they won't be re-elected.'

I couldn't see the connection. He thought he could have that much impact on an election? Who did he think he was? I thought he was dreaming and talking absolute nonsense. I had heard some random, far-fetched ideas about all sorts of things in my short twenty years, but this was something else! What planet was he from?

He talked about his time of being on the run, how he had initially spent time in the city, but became nervous as there were too many cops around, hence his move to continuing his life on the run in Gippsland.

One of the amazing admissions that also came out during this discussion was where Eastwood had been that morning. He'd first gone to Allambee South State School to kidnap that teacher and children, but on arriving found more cars and personnel at the school than was normal. Or at least, more than he had bargained on. It was confirmed at a later date by the head teacher of the school, Mr. Bill Blomeley, that they had two visiting Education Department advisors there that morning. Allambee South is about twenty kilometres north-east of Wooreen. Like Wooreen, Allambee South was a school with only one teacher, but with one more student than we had. Allambee South was one of the schools in our cluster that we were scheduled to meet with on a regular basis at Hallston, for Group Days.

If Wooreen was considered to be remote at eleven kilometres from the nearest major town, that being Leongatha, then Allambee South was considerably more isolated. Situated in the middle of the Strzelecki Ranges, it was more out of the way than Wooreen. It was over thirty kilometres from Leongatha. It was closer to Mirboo North, however, and right on the Grand Ridge Road, all of which would have certainly suited Eastwood's purposes.

Eastwood went on to explain that he had then tried to go to his second choice of schools, Hallston State School. Hallston is about ten kilometres north of Wooreen. In heading to Hallston, Eastwood took a wrong turn and ended up at Wooreen by mistake!

Upon arrival at our school, Eastwood still thought he was at Hallston. It wasn't until some discussion with the children and me at the school that to his surprise, he found out that he was in fact at Wooreen State School. Hallston had fifteen children and a second teacher, a part time aid. I wondered what would have happened if he had turned up there.

Unbelievable! Lucky us!

With the chatter and an extended period of calm, I began to relax somewhat. The children seemed happy enough. The girls had bonded with the ladies brilliantly. The boys were happy to sleep in the van. Weighing up the situation, it appeared that Eastwood wasn't planning on shooting any of us; certainly not in the immediate future. He seemed quite amicable at this time, chatting and smoking a steady stream of cigarettes. The guys around me continued to give me comfort. Although the truck drivers weren't overly talkative, we chatted in quiet voices with the person next to us about the situation we now found ourselves in, as well as various other normal things, like our families, jobs, past experiences, sport and the like.

Greg and Ian explained how their families would be totally mystified as to where they were. Their families would have been making enquiries as of about 7.00pm that evening. We agreed that by this stage the police would have pieced together that their missing presence and the accident site were linked to the missing children and teacher from Wooreen.

The radio gave us news bulletins on the hour. It appeared that Eastwood was hoping to hear news of himself and his daring feat. It was like he was sitting back getting ready to enjoy the unfolding of the story, with the essential ingredient of the media giving him publicity. The seven and eight o'clock news bulletins came and went. Nothing was mentioned of any children missing from a remote school in South Gippsland.

The Eagles and America were popular bands at this time and a number of their songs were played and replayed over those hours. I particularly remember *Hotel California* and *Muskrat Love*. Another song that was played over and over was *Winter in America is Cold* by Doug Ashdown.

The interesting thing about those songs is that whenever I have heard them played since, my mind always goes back to those hours. The memories always come flooding back.

Then the nine o'clock news came on and we got a mention. It was only a small segment with a general statement to the effect that there were some children and a teacher missing from a school in Gippsland. It wasn't very encouraging.

Have they only just missed us? Haven't they sent out search parties yet?

It seemed like they didn't know that we'd been kidnapped, but that we were simply lost.

David, to my left, wasn't particularly talkative with me. He spoke mostly to his brother Robin, further to his left in a very quiet voice, most of which I could hardly decipher.

I said to him after hearing the nine o'clock news, 'Sounds like they don't know what's going on.'

Robin was listening to my comment.

'Don't worry,' Robin said. 'The whole place will be crawling with cops by morning. They know lots more than they're letting on. They will have seen the accident and they'll have a general idea where we are. This guy's stuffed! They'll be everywhere.'

He then added, 'Ted is destined for jail, where he belongs. We'll be fine.'

David nodded his head in agreement.

I found Robin's words most encouraging and full of promise.

I wondered what would be happening at the school and how the parents would be feeling. They would have been frantic with worry, I was sure. I wondered about my family back in Kyabram. Would they have been told of my missing state? What about Peter, my house mate? What would he be thinking and doing?

At ten o'clock the news was a little more forthcoming with the mention that police believed that the children and teacher from a school in South Gippsland had been kidnapped.

That's a bit better. At least they know we've been kidnapped and that I didn't just get the children and myself lost.

At eleven o'clock there was a much more comprehensive story of the kidnapping with Eastwood's, the children's and my names all included. The accident site on the Grand Ridge Road near English's Corner was also referred to, pointing to us being somewhere in the eastern part of South Gippsland. The news included the fact that my car and my wallet, watch and car keys had all been left behind at the school. Also, we learned that search parties had begun the hunt for us. The news report stated that Eastwood was reportedly on the run in Gippsland and that he was suspected of being involved.

This news bulletin was of considerable comfort. We knew that police and authorities were on their way. I also thought of the many different family members and friends who may have been listening to that broadcast and who would have been alarmed, upset and highly concerned about the children and me. I wondered if Mum and Dad or my brothers had heard it.

Eastwood suggested that police could search all they wanted, but they would never find us in such an out of the way place.

He stated, 'Don't get your hopes up, anyone. We're so remote here, they'll never find us.'

I was inclined to agree. Eastwood was enjoying this. I had a sense that he was feeling very much at home.

During later parts of the night we could hear aircraft, a plane or two and a helicopter, that we hoped were on the lookout for us. How they might see us in the dark puzzled me.

I had no jumper so I was thankful for the warm night. I was still wearing the filthy shirt that I'd been in all day. Each of us blokes had a blanket that we were able to half lie on and half put over us. Otherwise, there were no home comforts out here.

Hours went by. The children slept. The women seemed to sleep. Their chatter with the children had gradually abated over the hours and totally ceased about 11.30pm, I estimated. Periodically, Eastwood prowled around with a torch inspecting all his captives, especially the men. He walked over towards the tree, shining his torch at each of us. What did he need to check? It didn't seem to me that we were able to go anywhere.

I didn't want to sleep and nor could I. It appeared that Ian was nodding off. The other guys were noticeably awake. It seemed like sleep would completely elude most of us. David and Robin continued to talk very quietly with each other.

A LONG NIGHT

That night was an eventful period of time on a number of other fronts too.

There was no sleep for much of the Wooreen community, I later learned. Families and friends kept vigil. The parents of my nine students were going through hell.

At 3.30pm that Monday afternoon two of the parents from separate families, a dad and a mum, arrived at the school in their respective cars to pick up children. From their perspective, nothing looked out of the ordinary as they waited at the front gate for the children to come out. They could see the school building. Some children's bikes were still out the front ready to be cycled home. The rear of my car could be seen at the back of the school. They waited.

After ten minutes of waiting, one of the parents got out of their car and approached the school room. It was beginning to rain. Aiming to give the teacher a hurry up, this parent walked straight into the school building. They walked through the outside door and then through the classroom door. It was then that they noticed there was no one there.

There was silence. The room was void of anybody. The mother got quite a shock.

She had a quick look around. It was very surprising to her that no one would be in the school. She walked back outside and saw the notice on the front door:

HAVE GONE ON A NATURE
STUDY TRIP, WILL BE BACK
IN ONE HOUR!

She thought this notice was a little strange – particularly that it was not signed.

She went back out to the front gate to let the other parent know of our absence and of the words on the note. She then walked around to the back of the school building, past my car, to see if we could be seen in that direction. Nothing! She then walked back inside the building to have another look around. She noticed my watch, wallet and keys. She thought this to be even stranger.

She then went back to the other parent and conferred. They both decided to drive off in opposite directions to see if they could see us or speak to someone who might have seen us.

At this stage they must have been only mildly concerned, as well as partly annoyed that the children weren't ready for pick up.

Both parents arrived back at the school having found out nothing. They walked back into the school and heard the phone ringing. They answered the phone only to find that it was silent. Nothing could be heard from the ear piece. It seemed to be dead.

Much later I was to find out that although Eastwood had torn out the speaker from the phone's ear piece, ensuring that nothing could be heard when the phone was picked up and placed to a person's ear, it was still possible to make a telephone call and be heard at the other end of the phone.

The two parents, a little troubled by these events, waited at the school and continued to discuss the situation.

It was approximately 4.00pm.

Then another mother arrived. She explained that she had just rung the school to ask why her child wasn't home yet. She had heard a voice answer at the school but she hadn't been able to make herself heard. She was wondering what was going on.

The parents decided to go back to the nearest parent's home and phone various people in the district to see if anyone had seen, or if anyone knew anything about where the children and teacher might be. This drew total blanks. No one had seen us anywhere.

They decided to search some more. While two of the parents looked in different directions, one of the parents drove to Moss Vale Park, the only piece of natural bushland in the near vicinity suitable for a 'Nature Study Trip', to see if the children and teacher were there. No one found any hint of the children or teacher from the various directions travelled. They were all mystified.

The three parents briefly assembled at the school again. They couldn't understand it. As parents, they hadn't been notified of any excursion and that was the standard procedure. No one had seen us walking around the nearby farms. It wasn't a normal practice to walk around the farms anyway and they knew that if we had done that we would have been seen. There were only dairy and beef farms in the immediate area, with nothing particular to explore and we weren't at Moss Vale Park.

They thought that the note written in capital letters was a little strange. One parent said, 'Don't primary teachers write in lower case letters with capitals in just the appropriate places?' They also wondered why such a note would be written on a scrap of cardboard.

The parents re-entered the school room. They saw that some of the children's bags were still there but no lunches remained. Books, belongings and the remnants of some play lunches were just lying around and on top of the desks.

They must have questioned my integrity and wondered about their brief meetings with me. Was Robert reliable? Was he reckless? Why would he take the children walking around farmland anyway?

One parent commented about my car being out the back and how strange it was that my watch, keys and wallet were all left on my desk. They saw the classroom clock stopped at 11.10am. These things, along with the dead phone, made them particularly concerned.

They wondered what on earth was going on. Alarm bells rang. Pulse rates and blood pressures started going through the roof.

At 4.30pm they drove to the nearest farm house and rang the Leongatha police.

Initially, the parents received a nonchalant response to their phone call. The police wanted to know the times that the children had last been seen, how many children were missing, the name of the teacher, what kind of state the school was in, any unusual signs and more.

The police must have wondered at first what sort of a foolish teacher would get their children lost in farmland around Wooreen. Surely there was a logical explanation.

The police arrived at the school at 4.50pm. Stepping into the classroom, Sergeant Graham Washfold of Leongatha police took special notice of my watch, keys and wallet on the teacher's desk. That, along with the dead phone, the stopped clock, and the general state of the school quickly persuaded him to conclude that he was at a crime scene. He recognised a number of similarities to the Faraday kidnapping that he had been loosely associated with. He also searched the premises for more of the type of cardboard that had been nailed to the door, but none could be found. This pointed to the presence of an intruder who had brought in the piece of cardboard.

Soon the Wooreen district was buzzing with activity. D24 (the Victoria Police Mobile Communications Centre) at Police Headquarters in Melbourne was informed about the situation and things really started to liven up. A police guard was stationed at the front door of the school debarring anyone other than police personnel from entering. The Leongatha Ambulance was put on standby. Sergeant Washfold rang his neighbouring inspector James Cuzack at Meeniyan Police Station for support. Before long there were searchers numbering in the hundreds, made up mostly of volunteers from the Wooreen and Leongatha district.

The D24 mobile van arrived at 7.45pm. Police aircraft began searching from the air. Police Search and Rescue Squad units along with the Police Dog Squad were deployed to the area. More than sixty police were reported to be involved in the search. Local farmers on farm bikes and horses, as well as a local pony club, joined the effort. A radius of ten kilometres from the school was thoroughly searched. One report suggested that it looked like the whole of Leongatha had come out to Wooreen, such was the impact of what was taking place. Sergeant Washfold was to work over thirty hours straight without a break.

A vigil was kept at the school all night by a combination of police, parents and community members. Police set up a communications base in the classroom. Some local women served food and drinks that they and other members of the local community had brought in. Numerous tents were set up in the school ground to give the rescuers some rest.

Emergency phones were installed in the school. Extra lighting was connected. The grounds were flood lit. A media caravan was set up in the yard. Reporters were everywhere, interviewing, photographing, videoing, writing and broadcasting.

The little community of Wooreen was swamped. The only time that the little school saw more than small numbers of people was at election time since the school was always used as the local polling booth. What was happening now was way beyond that.

My District Inspector Mr. Ray Bull was called to the school at 7.00pm. He assisted police with the enquiries and joined in the watch with the parents.

Later that night the parents were sent home to rest with the promise that they would be contacted if there were any developments. There was very little rest and certainly no sleep for those poor parents. The anguish and trauma of not knowing where their precious children were, and worse still, that they had been kidnapped by the Faraday kidnapper, must have ripped them apart.

The police continued to work vigilantly all night, trying to piece together all the information.

>>><<<

All afternoon Neil Waack from Boolarra, working at the logging site in the forest at Womerah in the Tarra Valley, wondered why Robin Smith and Greg Peterson hadn't returned for more loads of logs. He'd said goodbye to Robin at about one o'clock that afternoon, after an extended conversation about some local news regarding the Boolarra General Store having been broken into.

At about 4.30pm he headed for home along the Grand Ridge Road. At approximately 5.00pm he came upon the back end of Robin's timber jinker next to a beaten-up Dodge utility, forming a formidable road block on a sharp corner, just short of English's Corner. He got out of his vehicle to inspect the scene.

He noticed enough strange things at this deserted site to make him sure that something disturbing had taken place and that it needed to be reported to the police. Besides the obvious signs of an accident he noticed the precarious position of the utility hanging over a massive drop, children's school bags, a crate of partly drunk milk in a very messy rear part of the utility, doors of both logging trucks wide open, with keys still in the ignition. An axe lying on the ground at the rear of Robin's truck heightened his sense of alarm.

Using a back track through the forest that he knew, he continued on his way to Boolarra, arriving home a little before 6.00pm. He immediately phoned the Boolarra police station. He was unable to make the resident policeman see the need for any action.

Frustrated, but not giving up, Neil rang the Churchill police station. Senior Constable Ronald Hateley was all ears. Senior Constable Hateley, having already heard that children were missing from the Wooreen State School, realised there was probably a connection between the two events. He promptly reported the information to higher authorities. It was approximately 6.20pm.

Still not fully understanding what had happened to his truck driving friends, Neil made numerous phone calls to contacts and hospitals that evening trying to work out where the men were. It wasn't until he heard a news bulletin later that evening that he was able to make better sense of what he'd seen and reported.

>>><<<

There was little sleep for the Assistant Commissioner of the Criminal Investigation Branch, Mr. Mick Miller, or the Victorian Acting Premier and Education Minister, Mr. Lindsay Thompson, that night. Mr. Miller, although he'd been alerted earlier, rang Mr. Thompson at 7.30pm to let him know that the teacher and nine children of Wooreen Primary School near Leongatha were missing and believed to be kidnapped by Eastwood, as the signs were so remarkably similar to Faraday. Much of the night, for Mr. Miller and Mr. Thompson, was spent at police headquarters, waiting on news and giving press conferences. At 6.00am the following morning they headed to Moorabbin Airport to board a helicopter bound for South-East Gippsland, but due to bad weather weren't able to leave until 7.15am.

>>><<<

There was no sleep for my parents, Jack and Dorrie, that night at their home in Kyabram. Police had given them the 'third degree' over the phone, as to the character of their son. Since I was only twenty years of age and so new to both teaching and the Gippsland area, I was an unknown quantity. Police needed to check out all possibilities. The phone rang hot. Mum had to vouch for my integrity, stability and maturity. My brother Ian was also questioned at length by Mr. Thompson. Was Robert a sensible young man? What sort of character is he? Has he ever been in trouble with the law? Was he a good student? Describe his behaviour. Who can you name that will vouch for his character?

Needless to say, the whole family were all highly anxious with the news. There was much prayer for the children and me and deep concern over the possibilities of what was happening. Mum and Dad were highly strung in nature and this scenario did not play out lightly for them. They waited and prayed with much anticipation. They listened to news bulletins on the hour, hoping for something positive.

>>><<<

Robin Smith's wife, Theresa, with four small children at home in Devon North, only about twenty kilometres as the crow flies from our camping site, was not overly worried at first about her husband's absence that Monday evening. He had occasionally broken down in his truck far from home and she assumed this was more than likely the case once again. She made some phone calls to various people asking if they knew anything about Robin's whereabouts. She rang Neil Waack. Not wanting to worry Theresa, Neil didn't tell her some of the details of what he knew.

Theresa had eventually gone to bed only to be woken at about 4.30am by police telling her that her husband had been kidnapped, along with the teacher and nine pupils from Wooreen Primary School.

Theresa was stunned.

Police explained to her that Robin's two trucks had been found near English's Corner, blocking the road. At the same site was a smashed-up Dodge utility, with some of the Wooreen children's school bags.

Theresa was left to worry herself sick.

>>><<<

Councilor Mat Gay, the President of the Alberton Shire, who owned the house that Robin and Theresa Smith were residing in, received a phone call from Yarram police at about 4.00am on Tuesday morning. The call was to let him know that Robin and David Smith, along with Greg Peterson, were missing and were believed to be mixed up in the kidnapping of the children and teacher from Wooreen. Soon after, two police officers, Sergeant Maurice Bradsworth and Senior Constable Brian Malone arrived at Councilor Gay's house to interview him about the missing persons.

>>><<<

My house-mate Peter didn't sleep that night. He arrived home at about 6.00pm on Monday from his day of teaching at Coalville to find numerous police at our Couper Street house in Mirboo North. He was dumbfounded as to what on earth was going on. The police wanted to know all about me, from Peter's viewpoint. Anything strange? Anything out of the ordinary that morning?

Was Robert Hunter reliable? Honest? Reckless? They inspected the house, my bedroom, the bathroom, my toiletries and particularly my shaving gear. Why my shaving gear? I had an unruly red beard. Perhaps they wanted to make sure that I hadn't been shaving, confirming that my beard was genuine? I don't know.

Peter promptly went in search for me also. He drove to Wooreen, where he found what seemed like thousands of people. He couldn't find a parking spot nearby so he parked about a kilometre away and walked to the school. He spoke with parents and community members and the police again, saw my car and the school room overtaken by more people than he could imagine. He couldn't believe it.

Eventually he went back to our house at Mirboo North and found that sleep escaped him.

>>><<<

Two of the children's dads were on a fishing trip at Bermagui in New South Wales and were not contactable. They'd had a good night's sleep knowing nothing of their wives' despair or their children's plight. At 6.30am on Tuesday morning, as they were about to get on a boat to go out fishing for the day, they were approached by two policemen. After confirming their identity, they were told that their two children had been kidnapped by a gunman. Shocked, they immediately chartered a light aircraft to fly them straight home.

ESCAPE: TUESDAY 4:00AM

In the early hours of Tuesday morning, in our remote camping spot nearly two hundred kilometres east of Wooreen in the bush near Woodside, the children slept while the adults continued to listen to the radio. Eastwood from time to time got up and checked on us, shining his torch on his prisoners to make sure everything was in order.

At around four o'clock in the morning I must have drifted off to sleep along with most of the other men.

But not Robin Smith!

Robin was wide awake with heart thumping and adrenalin rushing.

Although Eastwood had watched us all lock the chain around our wrists, Robin's subtle twisting of the chain had done the trick. Once untwisted, Robin had a bit of extra slack in the loop. In the early hours of the morning he was able to force his hand out from the bonds of the chain. Robin was ready to escape when the time was right.

With his hand free, Robin waited and waited and waited, hoping and praying that Eastwood would doze off so that he could sneak off to get help. He had strategically positioned himself on the opposite side of the tree from where Eastwood was lounging on his reclining deck chair. He had partly found himself in that position by good fortune and partly by a little bit of manoeuvring. He had shuffled himself and the rest of us guys around a little so that he was obscured from Eastwood's sight by the broad trunk of the tree.

He hadn't mentioned anything about his intentions to me, positioned further down the chain, with David in between. I was totally unaware of his hand being free, what he was planning on doing and what he was about to go through.

How his heart would have raced knowing that he was free of the chain and able to move away from Eastwood. Waiting. Waiting. Hoping. Praying. Waiting for the opportunity to creep away.

With his heart pounding and his adrenaline pumping, there was no way he could have fallen asleep by mistake.

He kept on listening for stirrings from Eastwood. Being obscured by the tree was both a help and a hindrance. He couldn't be seen by Eastwood easily, but nor could he see Eastwood – whether he was asleep or not. Robin was hoping that the wind would spring up to create enough noise in the trees to cover up the sound of his movement. Eventually he ascertained that it was time to move. It seemed like most or all of us, including Eastwood, were asleep. Some snoring. Perhaps enough snoring to dull his furtive movements. He took off his boots for a quieter getaway. And then with footwear in hand he crept. Very slowly at first. Hoping against hope that Eastwood wouldn't be alerted. Highly aware of the noise the twigs and sticks and leaves were making, snapping and crunching under his feet, he continued his stealthy creeping.

Would Eastwood hear him?

Would Eastwood wake up?

Would he be shot?

Robin Smith was risking his life for us.

I'm sure that if Eastwood had woken up at that moment, he would have shot Robin. Robin's heart must have almost exploded with the height of the moment.

For what Robin was doing, I was and will be eternally grateful.

Robin's course of escape took him past the sleeping students and the two women. Having crept no more than ten steps from his resting place, he came across one of the older girls half sitting up, looking directly at him, with wide eyes. The girl's mouth was open, ready to speak to Robin. Alarmed that the girl may awake the gunman, Robin quickly put his fingers to his mouth signalling a 'Shhh'. Thankfully the bright-eyed little girl lay back down without a sound.

Relieved that a possible warning to Eastwood had been averted, Robin moved onward creeping on his haunches towards the narrow track. Once he had passed the van, having the vehicle between him and Eastwood, Robin felt a certain amount of protection. And then he was far enough away to run. After a few metres he stopped to put his boots back on and then he ran again. He ran as fast as he could. Then he slowed down to a jog to conserve his energy.

It was almost ten kilometres from our camping spot to the South Gippsland Highway where he knew there was the farm house. The same farm house that I had seen the previous evening, although I would never have known where to find it.

He steadily jogged the entire distance. He didn't stop. He didn't walk.

Robin's intention was to get help while it was still dark and to get back to us before Eastwood woke up.

Panting and out of breath, he reached the front door of the house and started knocking, banging, yelling, trying to raise the sleeping household. Eventually one of the children in the family woke and went to the door. Robin, in an agitated state, struggled to express himself.

'Ring the police!'

'Just ring the police!'

The child woke the father. The father had very limited English, being a relatively new Australian. This man could not work out what was going on so early in the morning. He was quite wary of the police and refused to ring. He had no understanding of what the desperate need was. Further pleas from Robin still fell on non-understanding ears.

Precious minutes were being wasted. Could he get these people to understand him?

The man's older daughter came to the door to find out what all the fuss was about. She could speak English very well. Robin was able to explain the situation to her. She had heard the news and was aware of the kidnapping.

The call was made to the Yarram Police Station. Marg Bradsworth, the wife of Sergeant Maurice Bradsworth, was at home to answer the call, as her husband was out with Senior Constable Brian Malone interviewing Councilor Mat Gay. She promptly rang her husband, letting him know that she had an agitated Robin Smith on the phone and that he was at the farm house at the end of Boundary Road on the South Gippsland Highway. Further phone calls were made. Sergeant Bradsworth and Senior Constable Malone rushed to the farm house.

Help would be on its way.

I remained asleep.

Police officers Bradsworth and Malone sped to the farm house to pick up Robin. They wasted no time in ringing D24 and letting Police Headquarters know that one of the truck drivers had escaped from the kidnapper. They passed on the information of where Eastwood, the children and the teacher were. Robin then began to direct the sergeants to our exact location.

>>><<<

I was woken up by two of the guys whispering near me. Greg was asking David where Robin was.

I looked to see a space where Robin had been.

He had vanished! Snuck off in the brief time that we had been asleep.

'How long ago did he leave?'

David was not forthcoming with a direct answer. Did David know more than he was letting on?

It was early dawn. Perhaps 6.30am. There was a light breeze blowing. The trees were making a steady rustling sound. I could hear music from the radio.

Eastwood had evidently fallen asleep and was still asleep! *Long may it last.*

Had Robin been gone long enough for us to expect help soon? Were we going to be saved? These were the big questions on our lips. There didn't seem to be any answers.

I had only a vague idea of how far it would have been to the nearest house. Would Robin have been able to ring the police? Would they be able to locate us?

Lucy was beginning to do the rounds with her chocolate again. She noticed Robin's absence. 'Where is he?' she asked. 'Shh!' was the signal. Index fingers were raised to lips.

Some of the other children and the women were stirring and had also noticed Robin's absence. They exchanged quizzical looks.

Everyone stayed quiet. Expectant.

We waited. What now?

On the radio we heard a special news bulletin, all about the kidnapping. The radio was giving lots of accurate detail, similar to the 11.00pm news the previous evening, but more. Three of the men from the trucks were named.

Then Eastwood woke up.

He too was listening to the news bulletin.

The report mentioned the general area in South-East Gippsland, where they believed us to be. People were asked to be on the lookout. Anyone with any information was asked to call a particular phone number.

Ron, Russell and Dale had woken and come over from the van to join the girls and the women.

Eastwood began to get up.

Slowly at first, he rose … stood … stretched, and began to walk towards us captives … looking … checking … commenting how he fell asleep …

Ron, oblivious to the fact that Robin was missing and the tension of the moment, had practical matters on his mind. He must have been puzzling overnight about similar logistics to the rest of us. He asked Eastwood, 'How are you going to get wherever you want to go?'

'I've got a special way,' was the answer.

Although none the wiser, Ron let the issue sit.

We held our breath.

What was going to happen here? Would he notice straight away?

He walked over towards us men, keeping a safe distance, until he was in view of the space. Then he saw the empty hole and the tell-tale evidence of the unoccupied chain.

With great agitation, 'Where's Singlet?'

We all shook our heads.

'How long has he been gone?'

Again, we shook our heads.

Eastwood went nuts! He was worried. He knew he'd blown it!

'Shit! Fuck him!'

'Get in the fucking car! All of you! Now!'

This was a very tense moment. We were all fearful for our lives. If anything else went wrong, if any of us had crossed him, I'm sure bullets would have been fired.

Hearts raced! Adrenalin pumped!

Everyone did what they were told.

With much yelling and cursing he undid the chain from around the tree and hurried us all over to the van. Pulled the tarp off. Shoved us all into the van. This was all in a matter of seconds. Everything except us captives was left behind. It was no easier to fit in the van this time than the last, even with one less person. No extra tying of chains to the vehicle. Just get in and go.

Three boys squashed in the front again. The rest of us sandwiched in the back. I found myself sitting behind Eastwood's seat, slightly to the left. My seat allowed me to see out the front window. Behind me was the bunk bed. Muriel was lying on the top bunk. There were only centimetres between her head and the roof. Anticipating further crazy and life-threatening driving, she was putting a motor bike helmet on her head. How a motor bike helmet came to be there at that moment I have no idea. I hadn't seen it before.

Off we set. Wheels skidding, van sliding and slewing all over the place, like mad things we headed along that small dirt track that we had been on the previous afternoon. We sped through the small gap in the bushes. We bounced over the erosion and pot holes. We slurred over the road and along this roughest of dirt tracks.

It was approximately 6.45am. It was quite light.

We came to the sandy gravel road that we had turned off last evening and turned left.

We sped around bends and corners at breakneck speed. Some of this road had extensive straight stretches which allowed Eastwood to drive even faster.

He continued to utter curses and expletives.

My pulse rate was going through the roof. This was crazy! The children and I had nearly all been killed in the utility only hours before. Now it was happening again, but this time Eastwood was totally out of control. Once again, I was scared for my life! And, of course, for the children's lives.

We were heading back towards the South Gippsland Highway.

About six kilometres along the road we saw a police car approaching from the opposite direction. Its bright lights were flashing and its siren was blaring.

Thank you, God! We've been rescued!

I had never been so happy to see the police in all my twenty years!

Naively, I thought that would be it. We had been found. Eastwood would stop the car. Get out and surrender and we would all go free. Not so.

That police car carried Robin Smith and Mat Gay, the local shire president, with policemen Maurice Bradsworth and Brian Malone, the local Yarram policemen.

Sergeant Bradsworth signaled for Eastwood to stop.

Eastwood ignored the demand and continued on driving like a maniac, passing the police car. He immediately turned off the road to the right onto what he thought was another minor track which turned out to be nothing more than an empty paddock. More expletives! He quickly turned around, wheels spinning all the while and sped back to where we'd turned off the road. He turned right, back onto Boundary Road, and continued on his way heading toward the South Gippsland Highway. By this time the police car had also turned around and was only some metres back on our left as we came out of the paddock. They followed us at a distance of thirty to forty metres, with lights flashing and sirens blaring.

I found out afterwards that this first police car on the scene had neither radio nor weapons! Not much help!

When we reached the highway we turned left. Off we sped in a north-easterly direction towards Sale, with a number of police cars on our tail. More police cars had arrived from behind, from the direction of Yarram. Eastwood was driving as fast as the Kombi could go. We had only gone a few kilometres when I saw another police car approaching in front. Now police were behind us and in front of us! All with lights flashing and sirens blaring. We hurtled onwards at full speed passing the approaching car. So, the pursuit continued.

As captives, we were intensely aware of the danger we were in. The chances of a collision seemed high. Someone noticed that the boys in the front didn't have their seat belts on. I leant over the front seat and told the boys to put them on. Dale, sitting next to Eastwood, was able to do this immediately. His was a lap seat belt. Ron was sitting next to the door with Russell next to him. Ron started tugging on his belt, trying to get some length to go around him and Russell. There was no length. It was jammed somewhere. We then realised that it was hanging out the door. We considered leaving it as it was. But Joy decided that we should get Ron to open the door a little to retrieve the rest of the seatbelt. He did this. But after repeated attempts, he was unable to get the door to shut properly. We were going at maximum speed. It seemed that the air pressure in the car was working against his attempts to close the door. It remained only half shut. So, we told Ron to lock the door, which he did. The seat belt was eventually secured around both Ron and Russell.

On we sped.

An approaching plain sedan repeatedly flashed their head lights at us as we approached, as if to say, 'Stop! Or slow down! You've got police cars after you.' This car approaching and flashing their lights was just like the cars that had flashed at me on country roads in the past, in a friendly way, to alert me to the fact that there was a speed detector, or police ahead of me. It was always greatly appreciated. But now it seemed so out of place. Did they really think that we didn't know there were a number of police cars behind us? It was comical recalling this incident at a later date.

It wasn't easy to see behind us, with limited windows and twelve of us jammed in the back. But I was able to glimpse the fact that there were a large number of police cars following us from behind now. Where they had all come from, I wasn't quite sure.

It was just as I would have seen in a movie. I really couldn't believe this was happening to me. My stomach continued to be in knots and I was shaking all over.

Eastwood, holding his revolver in hand, put his hand and arm out the window while he was driving and took some shots at the police cars chasing us. I couldn't believe what I was seeing.

This guy is actually shooting at the police!

Ahead, I could see another police car approaching with lights flashing. It seemed to be slowing down and pulling over to its left, but then it turned hard, right across the middle of the road about seventy metres in front of us. It stopped in that position, in the centre of the road, forming a make-shift road block. A number of policemen appeared, one ran from the driver's side, around the back of the vehicle, rifle in hand, preparing to shoot. Eastwood was making no sign of slowing down. He then started to veer slightly to the side. Slowing down ever so slightly, Eastwood headed off the sealed part of the road towards the verge. This was the graveled edge of the road with a loosely graded slope down to the table drain.

Is he going to be able to maintain control of this van? Are we going to be hit by a bullet?

In anticipation of receiving shots to the vehicle, one of us yelled, 'Get your heads down!' We all ducked. Children and adults alike. We heard the shot but I was unaware of any impact.

As it turned out, ducking our heads was the opposite of what was needed. The policeman shot low, shooting at our front right tyre.

Eastwood drove the van along the graveled edge of the road with just the slightest skidding on the loose gravel. Somehow, he was able to maintain control of the vehicle, despite being so overloaded and driving at such a rapid rate. Steering slightly to the right, Eastwood drove the van back onto the bitumen.

In the back of the van we took stock. No one was injured. We were all petrified and on high alert. It was all happening so quickly.

All the while what seemed like a dozen police cars continued to follow us.

On we went for some kilometres, driving as fast as the van could go.

Eastwood called out to the women, 'Is there any pepper in the van? I need it to get away from the police.'

Joy and Muriel replied in the negative.

'Come on! Find me some pepper!' he demanded.

He made some reference to us having had it pretty easy so far.

There must have been some indication from the ladies that there was indeed pepper stowed away in a cupboard as Greg and Ian started to search cupboards. A pepper shaker was located and passed to Eastwood which he placed in his top pocket.

It escaped my imagination how some pepper in a policeman's face was going to help him escape from all these police.

Where are we going? How can he possibly get away? Give up man! Stop this nonsense!

With police cars at the rear, at least one more time Eastwood put his hand, gun and arm out the window and took some shots at the pursuing police cars. I was vaguely aware of one or more of the children crying.

We had travelled approximately eighteen kilometres along the highway. About twenty-five minutes had elapsed since Eastwood had woken up.

We could see in the distance another road block, this time with two police cars nose to nose and armed policemen and plain clothes police by the side of the cars. I could see a number of them. It looked like they were preparing to take aim at us with rifles. The car on the right had its boot open with a policeman getting something out from it.

Again, it seemed that Eastwood had no intention of stopping. Pure madness!

Hell! More shooting! We are on the edge here! God, help us!

Again, someone called, 'Look out! Heads down!'

Slowing down much more this time, Eastwood drove completely off the road. This time we were heading for the table drain. In this place the drain was little more than a shallow depression. Through this we drove, with the van bumping up and down, tilting and leaning violently from side to side. We were thrown to and fro, bashing up against each other and bounced up and down as we hit the bumps. Heads hit the roof as we ran over holes. There were screams and tears. It was very scary. It was crazy!

How are the police going to shoot such a fast and violently moving target? Will one of us be shot by mistake?

Amazingly, Eastwood maintained control of the vehicle, again.

Meanwhile, police with guns were taking aim.

We heard a number of gun shots. One of these shots, instead of hitting a tyre, impacted above the front tyre just below Eastwood's seat. The bullet went right through the door of the van and who knows where after that. How close some of the children or us adults came to being shot is anyone's guess.

The three boys sitting in the front seat were particularly vulnerable. They were in a more open situation than us in the back and they were so close to Eastwood, with his gun. Joy was very worried about Dale in particular as he was leaning forward, presumably to look at the police shooting at us. She leaned over into the front and pulled him back saying, 'Keep back Dale!'

I'm sure that if it hadn't been for all of us hostages acting as protective shields for Eastwood, the police would have riddled him with bullets.

At about this time Joy also yelled at Eastwood, 'Stop the damn van and let the children out, for God's sake!'

This plea fell on deaf ears.

Our very rough and tilting course continued back through the drain again and onto the road. This time, however, we could tell that something was not right with the van. One of the tyres had been shot through. The sound and feel of a flat tyre became very obvious and Eastwood had no alternative but to slow down to a stop. We found ourselves motionless in the middle of the road, a short distance past the road block.

'Okay, it's over,' Eastwood said.

With that he opened his door, stepped out of the car with his hands in the air and gave himself up.

The first pursuit vehicle on the scene was a green CIB car, driven by Detective Sergeant Stan McCullagh, with Sergeant

Ross Atkinson in the passenger seat. Very quickly and bravely they advanced upon Eastwood, securing his capture and our safety.

Inside the van we were all relieved, but still uncertain as to how safe we were. A number of the children were crying. We heard another gun shot. Then a man, a plain clothes policeman we assumed, tried to open the passenger door. He couldn't, as it was locked. Ron unlocked the door. The man, then being able to open the door, thrust his head inside with a gun at the ready, asking if there was anyone else working with Eastwood. We assured him that Eastwood had been working alone.

Some of the girls were comforted by the women in the back of the van. I spoke with the boys in the front asking if they were okay. They gave me reassuring smiles but with very startled and glazed expressions.

At last the side door was opened and we began to exit the van, we four men still chained together in our line. As I rounded the back of the van I could see Eastwood on the road, lying flat on his front with hands being handcuffed behind his back, surrounded by police only a few metres from his driver's door. There was a pool of blood on the road underneath Eastwood's legs. His right trouser leg was covered in blood below the knee. One policeman had his knee firmly planted in the middle of Eastwood's back. Another policeman was searching him, making sure he held no surprises.

The keys for our padlocks were extricated from his pockets and given to another policeman nearby. That policeman then began unlocking us four men from our chained state.

'Are you guys alright?' he asked.

'Yes, we're fine,' we answered.

'Happy to be alive!' I added.

My padlock was undone and the chain loosed from around my wrist.

Free at last!

My wrist felt light, loose and so easy to move. It was such a good feeling.

The children were being cared for by a number of friendly policemen. Somehow a milk van appeared and the milkman was persuaded by a policeman to give the children and adults a carton of flavored milk. Ironically, the same drink made available to the children at the beginning of the ordeal, although this time flavoured and cold! I gratefully accepted the offer, opened the carton with shaking hands and took a mouthful. It was very good! I thoroughly enjoyed the sweet, cool taste.

Eastwood was bundled off into the back of one of the numerous police cars accompanied by a number of burly detectives. I guessed he would be locked up in the nearest police cell and not given too many privileges for some time.

We stood around on the road for quite a while chatting with our rescuers, checking on everyone's physical state and reassuring the children that everything was okay. I expressed my gratitude to as many police as I was able to speak to. I found Robin Smith and thanked him for his heroics. Like many heroes, he brushed off the thanks with a dismissive smile, saying something to the effect of being glad that everyone was safe. He wanted to know what it was like back at camp when Eastwood woke up to the fact that he had escaped. I tried as best I could to explain the panic, my fear of someone getting shot and the quick getaway.

It was approximately 7.30am. The whole drama had unfolded over a period of twenty-one hours.

Day Nine at Wooreen was finally over!

SALE AND HOME: TUESDAY

We were ushered into police cars and driven to Sale police station.

On the way, between mouthfuls of milk, I chatted about the ordeal with the friendly policeman who was driving. He mentioned that there had been another road block being prepared further along the road, near where we were travelling at that moment: an extra safeguard if Eastwood had been able to get past the previous one.

Travelling in the police car, I indulged in some feelings of gratitude and reflection. The nervous energy that I'd expended over the day had left me feeling numb and exhausted. It was all over! We were safe. Everyone was alive. No one had been seriously hurt. Although we had all been badly shaken, and despite the tears, I felt the children were looking good. There had been smiles all round back at our rescue site and they had looked quite happy and relaxed mixing with the police and the women. In one sense, the only casualty was Eastwood, who had been shot in the leg. I felt so relieved. I was very thankful for the police, law and order and particularly for Robin Smith.

Ever since the event I have had very fond attitudes towards the police. Any police! The Victorian police in this instance did an outstanding job of rescuing us. That there were so many of them, well organised and prepared to put their lives at risk for us, I will forever be grateful. Over the years, like most people, I've had occasions where I've needed to be booked, fined or spoken to by police for a variety of reasons, both good and bad. They have always been pleasant, helpful and appropriate.

Above all, I was thankful that I had got through the whole drama without doing anything particularly stupid, something that I would have regretted for the rest of my life, such as putting the children at risk by grabbing the gun. I was also very thankful that my school class was still intact and that I had survived the first serious challenge of my teaching career.

Little did I realise that the effects of the ordeal would play out in my life and the lives of the children, for the rest of our days here on Earth.

The police and other personnel, whose company we now found ourselves in, could not have been more supportive and kind. They required statements to be made. We needed to eat and drink and to speak with our families. We were all physically and emotionally exhausted.

Upon our arrival at Sale Police Station phone calls were made to families. Parents and children were reassured that we were safe. I spoke with my mum who was deeply shaken and still really concerned. She, along with dad and the rest of my family, had gone through one of the worst nights of their lives not knowing. Amidst her tears, she expressed her relief and gratitude, knowing that we had been saved by the police from our reckless captor.

I was able to visit the bathroom, to perform some essentials, like washing my face and giving my filthy beard a good rinse, as well as gulp down some fresh clean water. Luxury!

One of the police personnel made me a cup of tea. This was greatly appreciated!

Mr. Lindsay Thompson, the Education Minister and Acting Premier, and Mr. Mick Miller, the soon to be appointed Chief Commissioner of Police, were both there at the police station. We spoke briefly. They both expressed their relief that we were all safe. They also thanked me for my part in the ordeal. Apparently, I had stayed calm and composed – their words!

A local motel owner was coaxed into feeding the children, Ian Webber and myself at his motel. I don't know where the other truckies and Joy and Muriel got to. Along with a few police personnel, the children and I walked the short distance to the motel and were soon seated in what seemed like first class comfort. It felt like we were kings and queens in the motel's dining room. We were all given a full breakfast of toast, bacon and eggs. The atmosphere was somewhat jovial. The children and I began to relax.

I'm not sure who paid the bill. It was probably Victoria Police.

The hours felt drawn out as we made our official statements at the police station – the lengthy process was often interrupted by phone calls to and from the station. Radio, newspapers and television wanted to speak to whoever was available. The requests seemed endless. The police were able to keep much of it at bay.

The police, the children's parents and I discussed how we would get back home. The parents wanted to come and pick the children up straight away. The police, wanting the children's statements made without their parent's interference, assured the parents that they would drive the children home very soon.

Sandwiches, snacks and drinks were provided throughout the day.

After quite a few hours the police did drive us back home. They continued to be very kind to us all. The children were well entertained, being allowed to play with the flashing lights and siren switches. All of the children seemed to be reasonably relaxed and surprisingly happy.

It was a good two-hour drive along the Princes Highway through the Latrobe Valley and then south towards Leongatha and back to the school. There were three police cars in the convoy. Some of the time, for the children's enjoyment, the police turned on the sirens. All the way the police lights flashed. The mood was relatively quiet. Everyone was exhausted. The policeman who drove me chatted about the ordeal that I had been through, asking questions and making comments about how ridiculous Eastwood's stunt was.

Our arrival back at 'my little school' was something that I was totally unprepared for.

Not that I had been prepared for any of what had happened over the previous thirty or so hours, but this was also a total surprise.

We arrived back at the school at about 4.30pm.

The school had been completely taken over. There were people everywhere! More police cars! Police and media vans. It seemed like hundreds of cars were parked along the sides of the road. There was even a helicopter on the oval! I couldn't believe it. The press was demanding more interviews. My District Inspector was there. A whole lot of people who I had never met had taken over my school and classroom. It seemed crazy! The whole district had come to our little school to witness the return of the kidnapped children and their teacher.

I hadn't realised, but this was indicative of what the place had looked like since the previous evening.

Parents and children were reunited. The displays of emotion from both the parents and the children, along with their tears at this meeting, baffled me. I'd been with the children over the two days and there had been only a few tears throughout that whole time. *So why the over the top, near hysteria now?* In my youthful naivety, I hadn't reckoned on the pain and anguish the parents had gone through in those hours, from 3.30pm Monday, till 7.30am Tuesday. From the time when they first noticed us missing till the following morning when we were reported to be safe and sound and in the care of police, they had gone through absolute hell.

Nor had I realised how deeply upset the children were underneath the surface, throughout the ordeal.

The parents' display of emotion is one of the aspects of the ordeal that I have reflected on a lot over the years. How much should we protect our children from the rawness of our emotions? How open and honest should we be about our true feelings?

Initially, I thought some of the parents should have controlled themselves a little more and protected their children from the severe anguish that they had experienced and were continuing to feel.

But as the years have gone by, and having experienced some of the anguish of being a parent myself, I realise that it is more easily said than done.

My house mate Peter was also there, ready to take me home. Bless him!

One of the families very kindly invited us to go back to their house for dinner, which we were only too happy to do. We relaxed in their lounge, chatting and playing with the children. I was still in my vomit stained clothes and my trousers with the patch cut out. I was untidy, dirty and exhausted. A shower and bed couldn't come quickly enough.

The evening television news bulletins caught our attention. The Wooreen kidnapping was the big story of the day and seemed to dominate each of the broadcasts. The broadcast included numerous interviews with the children, parents and me, as well as interviews with Mr. Mick Miller and Mr. Lindsay Thompson. Then there were the scenes at the school and the pictures of the South Gippsland Highway where the police chase had ended, and some footage of our camping spot. Everything seemed to get a mention. Some of the details of the events, particularly of the accident and the rescue, were totally inaccurate.

It was quite unbelievable and surreal to see and to hear pictures and stories on national television, of the nine children and of me, Robert Hunter, their teacher, in such dramatic circumstances.

The media coverage didn't stop. The story was on the front pages as full spreads on the Tuesday's and Wednesday's morning and evening newspapers (*The Herald* was an evening newspaper in Victoria until 1990). Television and radio news bulletins gave the story major attention. Stories, pictures and interviews continued for the rest of the week.

My District Inspector, Mr. Ray Bull, suggested that I should take the rest of the week off and return to school on the following Monday. I agreed to this, expressing my appreciation for his thoughtfulness.

Although I was dog-tired, I was unable to sleep that first night back in my bed at Mirboo North. The previous two days' events continued to play over and over in my head. One of the things that replayed was the realisation that I personally had been under suspicion by police. Before it was ascertained that we had all been kidnapped by a third party, there was the distinct possibility that I had taken the children away. I was affronted! How dare they doubt my integrity?

It wasn't until I took a step back and looked at it logically and objectively that I realised that this questioning of my character was perfectly understandable and even necessary in determining that someone else was the offender.

The next morning the press came knocking on my door. Peter answered a few questions and told them in an assertive manner to go away, stating that I was unavailable for interview.

Peter took that day off school and we went off to the La Trobe Valley and played 'Tourist' at the Open Cut Mine. We also visited the partly and soon to be fully demolished township of Yallourn.

I travelled home to Kyabram the next day. Once again phone calls and the press followed me. Even playing cricket on the Saturday for my home team Churches, in the Kyabram and District Cricket Association, the local newspaper reporters arrived wanting interviews and photos.

The cricket team's and my performance left a lot to be desired. It probably reflected both what I had just gone through and something of my state of mind. Playing against Wyuna, we chased their meagre score of 73. We were unable to match it. I was out for 0! Our team slumped to an appalling 7-32. I had performed slightly better with the ball during Wyuna's innings, managing to claim one wicket, with figures of 1-11.

One of the press releases over that week included the publication of Eastwood's ransom letter. It was printed in full in the *Sunday Observer*, just as I've recorded it in the story, but with one modification. On the first page of the letter Eastwood had originally written, 'I HAVE KIDNAPPED THE TEACHER AND PUPILS FROM THE ALLAMBEE STATE PRIMARY SCHOOL.' He had subsequently drawn a line through the word 'ALLAMBEE' and written 'WOOREEN' above it. Presumably he had made this change while I was on the floor of the utility, before putting it in the post at Mirboo North.

The enthusiasm of the press continued on day one back at school. The press was there wanting photos and interviews at 9.00am. Then again at numerous times throughout the year. They appeared for an excursion to Melbourne, the court case, the end of year concert and other random occasions.

PART FOUR

THE AFTERMATH

My first day back at school on the Monday was difficult for a number of reasons.

I had learned before I fronted for school that day that two of the eldest children would not be returning to Wooreen but would be going to the 'big school' at Leongatha, in preparation for Secondary School the following year. I was really disappointed to lose these two older children who I had already bonded with and who were excellent students. Under the circumstances, however, this was totally understandable. But with losing these two students, I wondered whether the school would remain open. Thankfully, the remaining families wanted their children to continue at the school and for the school to remain open with seven students.

This had been decided at a School Council meeting in my absence over the weekend. I had been encouraged not to attend the meeting, but to continue to rest up at home, in Kyabram. I had made it clear to the School Council and all the parents that I wanted to continue teaching at the school.

At school on the Monday, however, two more children were not present at the beginning of the day. Only five students were in attendance.

The press was there wanting interviews. Reluctantly, I allowed the reporters inside the school, but with the promise that they would only take a few photos and then leave.

Soon after I allowed the press into the school, the two children that I'd been expecting to be at school arrived with their parents to tell me the news that they too would not be returning. They would be going to a different school in Leongatha.

This meant that I was to lose four of the oldest children and that only five children would remain.

Again, I was very disappointed. I did my best not to show these feelings.

Unfortunately, there was no appropriate place to have a private discussion with the family. The press was inside at this point so I tried to have this discussion outside, away from everyone else. We moved away from the front door, further along the north side of the building. It was not an easy discussion for the family or me. The parents didn't want to tell me of their hard decision and I didn't want to hear it. Although they had decided it was best for their children to go to school in Leongatha, they didn't want to let the local school down. All of their older children had previously attended the school throughout their primary years so they felt a strong loyalty to the school. This made it difficult for them to cut off those ties. I tried to be as accepting as possible of their explanation. It was one of those awkward conversations.

The press noticed this meeting going on and typically took the opportunity to take ample photos. There were multiple photos of this delicate moment broadcast all over the papers the next day. This was a total invasion of our privacy.

It was at this point that I decided that I'd had enough of the press. From then on, my sense of cooperation with them was significantly reduced.

They continued to make moves for interviews at regular intervals. Often I complied, but always in a very guarded way. This has continued at various times ever since. Thankfully the occasions have become less and less.

>>><<<

On Monday November 7, 1977, Edwin John Eastwood, twenty-six years old, pleaded guilty before Mr. Justice Murray in the Melbourne Supreme Court to twenty-five charges, including sixteen counts of kidnapping, three counts of theft of a motor vehicle, three counts of using a firearm with intent to avoid lawful apprehension, one count of escaping lawful custody, one count of burglary, and one count of theft and other charges arising from the Wooreen kidnapping.

He was sentenced to a total of twenty-one years' imprisonment and his Honour indicated he would be eligible for parole after eighteen years.

He was officially released from jail in 1993.

FORTY YEARS ON

In February of 2017 a forty-year reunion was held with most of the Wooreen students of 1977 and their families. Robin Smith and his family attended, as did Greg Peterson's family, Graeme Washfold and numerous other policemen involved in the rescue.

This was the first time many of us had seen each other since the event. I had not kept in contact with the four students who had left the school after the kidnapping. Although I had completed the year at the school in 1977 with five students, after that year I had very limited contact with them as well.

The reunion was a momentous event. Sadly, a few of the students were unable to attend for various reasons. They were fondly remembered, along with Greg Peterson, David Smith, Ian Webber, Joy Edward and Muriel Deipenau.

Meeting up with so many of the players in the kidnapping was like being reunited with long lost relatives not seen for forty years.

In particular, no one had met up with Robin Smith, our hero and saviour, for forty years either. Meeting Robin again was like nothing I have ever experienced. We had all replayed the story over and over in our minds, remembering the unsung heroics of Robin. To see him again after such a long time brought on feelings you often only read about.

We all hugged him and shook his hand with outward displays of deep emotion, like a brother or father we hadn't seen for nearly a lifetime.

Sadly, Greg Peterson passed away in 2003. Thankfully many of his family were able to attend the reunion and some special connections were made between his family and many of us.

>>><<<

Over the years I have been asked numerous questions by people, including the press, as to how I have fared after the event and how I have been able to work through the trauma. These questions have often been asked in the knowledge that so many others in similar circumstances have developed severe health issues, mental health problems and serious emotional disorders.

Some of the most frequently asked questions, along with answers follow. The responses are explanations of what is true for me.

Did you continue teaching? Did the Education Department look after you?

I completed the year at Wooreen, teaching five children, with a new enrolment in the final term. It was a very good year, in the end. I loved the work. The children were terrific. The community was particularly supportive and I was pleased with the end results.

I continued teaching in Gippsland for the following two years in the Latrobe Valley.

In 1980 I enjoyed another year teaching at a rural school. I was placed at Ruffy in the Strathbogie Ranges in Northern Victoria. Ruffy was a two-teacher school and this time, although the name may suggest otherwise, my year was quite smooth.

I returned to the Kyabram area in 1981. I've continued to be employed by the Education Department up to the time of writing.

The late Mr. Lindsay Thompson was particularly caring, both immediately after the event and since. On a number of occasions, he contacted me for a chat enquiring of my welfare along with the children's. I very much appreciated his efforts and interest. One of the calls took place while I was living and teaching with my wife and children in England in 2003. The distance didn't stop him from reaching out.

Did you or the children receive counselling?

The children and I weren't offered any counselling. It wasn't the normal practice of that time.

I didn't debrief properly to anyone. My family and close friends asked questions, which I was only too happy to answer but there was never any in-depth revisiting the details of what had happened and so there was limited opportunity to get in touch with the feelings and thoughts that surrounded the trauma. My parents, like most people of the time, worked on the theory that the sooner a person got on with their life and forgot the ordeal the better.

Likewise, most of the students had limited opportunity to debrief.

In hindsight counselling would have helped considerably in the healing process. The expectation to get back on the horse, to grin and bear it, although in one sense may be helpful, by itself was unwise. Some of us have suffered because of that thinking. The need to properly debrief, talk through events, to be listened to at length and to get in touch with feelings is vital. Thankfully, today people have these opportunities available to them.

What do you think about Robin Smith's heroism? Did you keep in contact?

I've expressed much of my attitude towards Robin in the body of this story. I've added some other, more up-to-date thoughts in the chapter entitled Notes on Sources, from recent contact. But I need to reiterate, Robin Smith is a hero! Anyone who risks their life for their fellow man is to be greatly honored.

The words are often uttered at ANZAC and Remembrance Day ceremonies, 'No greater love has any man, than that he would lay down his life for his friends.' Very true words, first recorded as spoken by Jesus, and which He ultimately fulfilled. To this day, my two greatest heroes in life are Jesus Christ and Robin Smith. They're the only two people I understand to have put their life on the line for mine.

Regrettably I didn't keep in contact. In hindsight, I wish I had. We were geographically a long way apart and we continued on with our own lives.

The lack of ongoing contact with all of the players until the forty-year reunion is interesting. Some have expressed that this happened out of respect for the other people. It may also be to do with not being sure of how much others wanted to relive and discuss the event, so it was put in the 'too hard basket'.

As described at the start of this chapter, the reuniting of friendships recently has been enjoyed by everyone. It's been most refreshing and very healthy. The timing was right.

Do you think you have been able to overcome the effects of the trauma? How did you get over the trauma?

I think that I have been healed from the damage of the ordeal, but it wasn't immediate, it was a process. On occasions, the effects of the trauma have reoccurred. For instance, in writing the story in the detail that I have, I've experienced unnerving flashbacks, heightened levels of emotions and lingering thoughts. It seems this is very normal when revisiting a traumatic event to such an extent.

A number of factors helped with overcoming the trauma and experiencing healing.

From the time of the event I chose to be grateful for how everything had turned out. I had many things to be thankful for.

I continued to live an active life, reaching out to others wherever possible. Going back to school was an important part of this, as was my church involvement, my family and friends and sporting commitments. There was a temptation to become self-absorbed and to dwell on the events of the kidnapping in an unhealthy way, however staying outward focused helped overcome that tendency.

I trusted God with my life. I believed that He had me in His care and that He had a plan for my future. I also believed that my eternal destiny was safe in Him.

These things coupled with much of the content described in the following answer, left me with a strong sense of purpose and peace, which aided greatly in the healing process.

What were your feelings towards Eastwood?

What Eastwood did was terrible. It was disgraceful and totally unacceptable! However, knowing that I had been forgiven for all my mistakes and failings, I chose to forgive him.

I didn't approve of what Eastwood did. Not at all! It was a despicable act! We had been violated. But I couldn't allow a negative or angry attitude to rule my mind and life keeping me chained and captive. I had to let go of any inclination to dwell on his evil deed, on my own pain and on any vengeful tendencies that I might have had.

Forgiveness broke the chains that potentially would have kept me attached to Eastwood for the rest of my life. It set me free.

I understood that forgiving was different to forgetting. I wouldn't ever forget what Eastwood did, but I still needed to forgive him for what he did.

This allowed the healing process to continue unhindered.

If I had allowed a negative, spiteful or angry attitude to rule my thinking, in many ways I would have been lowering myself to Eastwood's level. I needed to rise above that. If I had let any of these negatives linger in my life they would have had an adverse effect on the person I have become. I may have become much like that which I disapproved of and I may well have grown bitter and resentful.

Love breeds love. Hate breeds hate. The only way to conquer hate is with love. That includes forgiving those that wrong us.

I believe my ongoing excellent general health, mental state and emotional wellbeing is largely attributable to God's healing and the above-mentioned beliefs and practices.

While writing this story and reliving Eastwood's evil deed, at times I've felt angry and resentful about what he did, but I've chosen to keep on forgiving.

Did you receive any compensation?

Yes, with an interesting twist.

My position, as described in the preceding answer, came to a head for me when the opportunity arose to apply to The Crimes Compensation Tribunal for compensation for the losses, injuries, stress and strain that we had incurred from the kidnapping experience. The parents all saw the need and wanted to take full advantage of the opportunity to apply for compensation for each of their children and they strongly encouraged me to do the same.

I didn't see the need for myself. I was thankful for the way things had worked out. Yes, there had been considerable losses and I had certainly experienced a lot of stress and strain; however, I didn't believe it necessary or right that I apply for this compensation.

In fumbling sorts of ways, I tried to explain this to the parents. Eventually, I succumbed to their pressure. Against my better judgement, I decided to apply for the compensation. Along with the families, I filled out the forms.

In going through the process of completing the application, I had a change of heart. I convinced myself that I deserved this compensation. I too had been traumatised and violated, so why shouldn't I claim compensation?

In due course, we were given an appointment day to have personal interviews with a judge in Melbourne at the Crimes Compensation Tribunal. My interview didn't last much longer than five minutes. The judge asked me to explain some of the symptoms of stress and strain that I had experienced. I described the palpitations, the sleepless nights, the thoughts that continued to replay over in my mind and the disappointment of the school being reduced to five children.

I was offered $1,000 by the judge. In 1977 that was a significant amount of money. For me it was close to two month's pay.

Regrettably, my response was, 'Is that all? Can't you give me more than that?'

It's amazing how selfish and money hungry I became in anticipation of a handout. The judge's response was polite but firm. He explained that was all he was able to allocate, according to set guidelines.

Twenty minutes into my journey home I had a car accident, colliding with a laundry van at the corner of Toorak and Glen Iris Roads. My car had to be towed away.

When I asked the panel beater what the cost was likely to be, he quoted me $1,000! The exact sum that I had just been awarded. $1,000 gone! Just like that.

That really made me sit up and take notice. I knew my motives for seeking compensation hadn't been right. I firmly believed all along that my attitude of being thankful and appreciative for all that had played out was the right way.

That is the only serious accident I have ever had in all of my more than forty-two years of driving!

NOTES ON SOURCES

When I began writing this account, thirty-nine years after the event, it soon became apparent that I had forgotten a lot of information. However, with extensive research, most of it came back to my memory. Many long-overlooked details were uncovered. A few of the many examples include:

- I had completely forgotten that Eastwood had chained me up initially, with the children in the classroom. I only remembered the tying up, blindfolding and gagging.
- Likewise, I had completely forgotten that I asked the children to all go outside and wave madly in an attempt to draw attention to our plight, while we were chained up and the kidnapper was getting his vehicle.
- I thought the second truck that came along at English's Corner was a tip truck. I subsequently learnt that it was not only another logging truck but Robin's second truck.
- I had completely forgotten that after the crash the children had to get out of the mangled vehicle through the side window, which Eastwood had to smash.
- I thought Robin Smith wore a white singlet. I am even quoted in my police statement that it was white. It was blue! Everyone I've spoken to says it was blue, even Robin himself! So much for the credibility of my observations!

Even after extensive research many things still remained blurred and obscure. Where these exist, I've had to come up with the most likely explanations. A few examples of these include:

- I had always thought there were three road blocks on the high-speed chase on the South Gippsland Highway. I've conceded that there may have only been two.
- I have little memory of where the kidnapper positioned himself when he moved us chained up men each time.
- The layout and seating positions when we were inside the Kombi.
- Many of the conversations between the children and me, with Eastwood, with the truck drivers and the women.
- The exact timing of some of the events.

The Victoria Police Museum have been particularly helpful in providing me with as much information and photos as was available. Most of this information has been included in the story. Some I mention now:

- Senior Constable Ronald Hateley of Churchill Police visited the accident site at English's corner on the evening of February 14. Included in his witness statement to the Crown is the following: 'On arrival I observed a grey coloured Dodge utility in a stationary position facing east, it was half off the road on the northern side and was in contact with a white guide post, which was the only object preventing it from falling down the very steep hill on that side of the road.'
- The bravery and heroism of many Victorian Police has continued to come to light. Fifteen individual police were given special recognition for their contribution. A large number of other police were ready to put their lives on the line to secure our safety and rescue also. They are all to be commended.

- Robin Smith's police statement included the following words: 'I was genuinely frightened and felt that he was serious and quite capable of killing all of us. The children were reasonably quiet and he appeared to be trying to keep them calm.'
- According to the late Greg Peterson's statement to police, our route from English's Corner to the camp site near Boundary Road firstly followed the Grand Ridge Road to Carrajung and beyond. We then followed the Carrajung-Woodside Road to the South Gippsland Highway at Woodside.
- My estimations of people's ages were not even close. I estimated that Robin and David Smith and Greg Peterson were much older than they were. The same was true for my estimations of Eastwood's age. In my mind, I thought they were all nearly thirty years of age. All were much younger, only a little older than me at twenty. Robin was twenty-five. David seventeen. Greg twenty-three. Eastwood twenty-six.

Interviews, conversations and statements from various police and other personnel involved in the drama have been included in the story, which has added significant detail and clarity. Here is some more information that wasn't easily included in the story:

- On Monday afternoon, February 14, Constable John Brookes of Sale Police drove to Korumburra to visit his parents. This meant driving through Mirboo North and Leongatha. His Senior Sergeant asked him to drop a letter off to Sergeant Graeme Washfold at Leongatha Police Station en route. He arrived at the

Leongatha Police Station at 4.40pm. As Constable Brookes approached the front door of the station, he met Sergeant Washfold making a hurried exit. Constable Brookes spoke to Sergeant Washfold explaining he had a letter for him from Sale police. Sergeant Washfold curtly told him to leave the letter at the door and that he was off to Wooreen to find nine missing children. Constable Brookes deposited the letter and continued on his way to have dinner with his folks. He completed the return journey back to Sale at 10.30pm ready for work the next morning.

At 5.00am on Tuesday morning Constable Brookes was prematurely woken by his Senior Sergeant calling him into work immediately. Along with Constable Doug Richardson and Constable Allan Callow they were instructed to get on the road and start calling at farm houses on the South Gippsland Highway heading towards Yarram. They were told to be on the lookout and instructed to ask the public if anyone had seen any suspicious activity or knew anything about nine missing children, a teacher and three truck drivers, all believed to being held hostage.

While performing the routine checks, having advanced as far as Stradbroke, at approximately 7.00am they received word to proceed immediately towards the Woodside-Darriman area where we had been located. They headed in that direction at top speed, travelling along the South Gippsland Highway. At approximately 7.15am they met the mustard Kombi Van driven by Eastwood with fifteen hostages aboard, approaching them from the direction of Woodside. They decided to intercept.

Constable Brookes was seated in the passenger seat when Constable Richardson drove their police car into the middle of the road, parking it across the highway, forming a road block. Very bravely, knowing that Eastwood was armed, Constable Brookes got out of the car, stood at the side of his car, faced the oncoming car and raised his hand as a command for Eastwood to stop. He was totally ignored. That was the first time he had ever been defied in his short experience with Victoria Police. He remembers ducking for cover at this point as Eastwood shot at them. He and his colleagues then gave chase, along with the other pursuing vehicles.

- At approximately 6.15pm on Monday February 14, Constable Peter Helms of Morwell Police was preparing to go home when his sergeant ordered him to drive to English's Corner to visit the site of a collision between a logging truck and a Dodge utility that was blocking the road.

Over the telephone, Peter recalled to me the precarious position of the utility hanging over the edge of the road with a massive drop beneath. Peter expressed to me how lucky the children and I were not to have plummeted over the edge. He explained how difficult it was for the tow truck to keep the vehicle on the road as the utility was being pulled away from the edge.

A lot of information was gained and confirmed at the time of the reunion and since, most of which has been included in the body of the story. A few others follow.

• The collision between the timber jinker and us, in Eastwood's stolen utility near English's Corner, was a complete game changer.

It was the moment where everything began to slowly turn in the children's and my favour. Up to that point Eastwood had everything on his terms. Although that collision in itself could have brought us to an unpleasant end, it became the catalyst for a whole range of events which eased our situation and saved us from many worse scenarios and potentially disastrous endings.

Robin highlighted the one or two seconds that would have made all the difference. The place and timing of that accident was impeccable.

English's Corner is the intersection of The Grand Ridge Road and Budgeree Road. It seems that Eastwood had almost exclusively driven us along the Grand Ridge Road to that point. The site of the accident was a sharp bend, about one hundred and fifty metres further east along the Grand Ridge Road from English's Corner.

That bend was the worst of its kind in the whole area and well known to the truck drivers. Robin explained how driving that bend took particular care. It involved a precise procedure which he'd had to execute on many occasions. It goes something like this: the previous bend was a blind bend. It involved driving out very wide, across the road, to the right and poking the nose of his truck over the dangerous edge, as far as possible. This was necessary in preparation to get around the next bend, 'our bend'. To execute our bend, he'd gone out as wide as possible again, to the left this time, putting his nose almost into the embankment so that his long tail wouldn't go over the edge of the road.

As he was performing this process he noticed our utility quickly approaching with Eastwood at the wheel. Eastwood waved at Robin as we passed him. Robin saw that Eastwood was travelling at a reckless speed and was aware that the utility would be unable to fit around the bend in the road as the timber jinker's logs and rear axle rounded the curve. Robin slowed down. Unable to see or realise the lack of space and the acuteness of the bend, Eastwood kept driving at a reckless speed. The collision resulted.

If it had been a second or two later, we would have missed hitting Robin's timber jinker and we would have continued on our way to Eastwood's camping spot without help, without company, without the angels and without our saviour.

I am extremely thankful for that accident, despite the devastating possibilities. Was God's protective hand on us, intervening? Were prayers answered that day in dramatic fashion?

- Robin explained another aspect of the accident of which I had no knowledge: what had happened after Eastwood had climbed out of his driver's door window, with the children mostly chained in the back and me still blind-folded and tied on the passenger floor.

When Eastwood approached Robin on the driver's side of the truck with gun in hand, Robin had only just climbed out of his truck. David, from his passenger's seat and through the back window of the truck's cabin, saw

Eastwood pointing the gun at Robin and telling Robin to get down flat on the road. David then quickly climbed out his door and started to run off up the embankment in a bid to escape. Eastwood called out for him to come back or he would shoot. David was a 'sitting duck' as he attempted to half climb and half run up the embankment. David continued in his efforts to escape. Eastwood told Robin to call him back. Concerned that David would be shot, Robin called his younger brother to return. Thankfully, David ceased his departure and joined his older brother. They were both then ordered to lie flat on the road next to the driver's door while Eastwood ripped the wires out from under the dash.

Eastwood was particularly concerned about the two-way radio that Robin had set up in his truck. He didn't want anyone being able to call for help or to communicate easily with the outside world. He wasn't particular about which wires he tore out. Apparently they were nearly all pulled out rendering the truck totally un-drivable.

• David's presence in the truck that day with Robin was a one-off. David was visiting Robin and family, with his parents. On impulse, he had decided to go trucking with Robin for the day.

• David had serious doubts regarding Robin's escape from our chained state around the tree. He tried to talk Robin out of escaping into the night. He was very concerned that it might all go terribly wrong.

AUTHOR'S NOTE

The first edition of *Day 9 at Wooreen* was a self-published effort in September 2018. I resorted to self-publishing after numerous knock backs from publishing companies. However, the day after I finished self-publishing, an article by John Silvester appeared in *The Age* endorsing the book which resulted in an offer from Wilkinson Publishing to publish it. So, in your hands you now have the retail edition of *Day 9 at Wooreen*, thanks to Wilkinson Publishing.

Much has happened since that first edition. The most significant was the Book Celebration that the Education Department of Victoria hosted in the Education Department buildings at 2 Treasury Place Melbourne in November 2018 (see photo pages). My Regional Director for North Western Victoria, Jeanette Nagorcka, was largely responsible for this taking place. Thanks Jeanette. Having received very little acknowledgement from the Education Department in 1977 it was both reassuring and fitting that they conducted such an event.

The Celebration saw everybody involved in the kidnapping either present or represented, along with many family and friends. Of special significance was locating Joy Edward (angel) and Ian Webber (hitchhiker in the second truck) and having them attend the event. After much searching, we were able to find Joy at 91 years of age, now Joy Butters, living in South Australia. Ian Webber was located in my 'backyard', in northern Victoria.

Sadly, Muriel Deipenau passed away in 2006. On a happier note however, a number of Muriel's family, including her sister Mavis, were able to attend the celebration.

Both Mick Miller's and Lindsay Thompson's families were also represented, with special reconnections made that are now ongoing.

The Education Department, Victoria Police and all present took the opportunity to applaud the heroism of Robin Smith. Each of the people involved in the kidnapping were acknowledged for the trauma experienced and the resilient character they have developed. *Day 9 at Wooreen* was recognised as playing an important role in the healing process and endorsed as a realistic account of the ordeal.

Finding Joy was special for a number of reasons. Of particular interest are the photos that she produced (see photo pages). She took these photos at the road side, immediately after our rescue. Joy had kept her camera well-hidden at the bottom of her bag during the kidnapping, for fear of having it confiscated by Eastwood. As can be seen, they are very raw and reveal much of the gravity of the ordeal.

The overwhelming positive feedback on the book, from everyone associated with the kidnapping, as well as the general public, has been far beyond my expectations. Similarly, the popularity of the seminar Kidnapped Teacher Talks – Health After Hurt has been significant and become a wonderful opportunity to support people in overcoming their pains and traumas.

Rob Hunter
March 2019

ACKNOWLEDGEMENTS

To my wife Judi, your love and counsel is out of this world. I'm indebted to you. Along with our children, you have encouraged and inspired me throughout this journey. Thank you so much! I love you more than words can say. Andy and Amy, Mat, Simon, Tim and Beth, thanks for cheering me on. You're the best!

Many thanks to my great friend Lance Marke, whose support from the very beginning was second to none. It is greatly appreciated. Lance, you're a ripper!

To the class of '77. Please forgive me if it seems like I continue to treat you as 'my children'. Maree, Leonie, Josephine, Laurene, Ray, Brett, Karina, Danny and Rohan: Thank you for your encouragement and interest in this book venture. Having been reacquainted with you of late, it's wonderful how much good has come out of a bad situation. Thanks for doing some hard yards with me, being prepared to rehash the drama. Thanks Ray for your endorsing words.

To Robin Smith, our hero. You are greatly loved. Thank you for all that you did back then and for continuing to motivate us all today. For your endorsing words too, thanks.

To the Victoria Police, thank you for saving us. Your efforts in February 1977 and always are greatly appreciated. Keep up the good work.

Mr. Mick Miller, thanks so much for your words, encouragement and support, back then, recently and here. You are a legend!

To all those who searched and helped in any way in our rescue. Your efforts and preparedness to put your lives on the line for us, were and continue to be greatly appreciated.

Leonie Smith, thanks for the visit that unlocked the gate. You're a honey!

To the Victoria Police Museum, thanks for all of your help and assistance with information, statements, pictures and exhibits. You have been particularly helpful.

To Jono Newmarch, editor number one. Thanks heaps, Jono. Your practical, emotional and smart advice, as well as all of your hard work has been marvellous.

To Julia Tulloh Harper, editor number two. You're a wonder! The fine tuning has been spot on and most appreciated.

John Hosking, for your proofreading, thanks so much and as always, your encouragement and inspiration is wonderful.

To the late Mr. Lindsay Thompson, a special thank you. To the Education Department of Victoria and all my colleagues over the last forty plus years, a big thank you to all of you. I've loved working with you.

Jacqui Naunton, you have great taste. The quality of your work is without question.

Kaden McDonell, thanks mate! I love your artwork.

Andrew Rule and John Silvester, thanks for your interest and help with this venture – your knowledge and input has been invaluable.

Wilkinson Publishing, Michael and Jess, thanks for believing in this story and seeing its possibilities, even after my self-publishing edition. A pleasure working with you.

To all who have supported me personally, not just with this project but in all sorts of different ways, thanks.

ABOUT THE AUTHOR

Following the kidnapping of 1977, Rob continued to work as a teacher with the Education Department of Victoria until February 2018. He is married to Judi and presently resides in rural Victoria. They have four adult sons.

Rob is the founder and presenter of the seminar Kidnapped Teacher Talks – Health After Hurt.

The Seminar is based on the health that Rob experiences despite the trauma of his kidnapping.

e: kidnappedteachertalks@gmail.com
w: www.kidnappedteachertalks.com

f Kidnapped Teacher Talks